HOT COFFEE AND COLD PIZZA FOR BREAKFAST

HOT COFFEE AND COLD PIZZA FOR BREAKFAST

Musings from the
Past and Present

To Melissa —

For your encouragement, support and caring of Jim and Carol, my dear friends.

Elaine B. Cameron

Elaine Cameron

Palmetto Publishing Group
Charleston, SC

Hot Coffee and Cold Pizza for Breakfast
Copyright © 2018 by Elaine Cameron
All rights reserved

First Edition

Printed in the United States

ISBN-13: 978-1-64111-140-9
ISBN-10: 1-64111-140-2

For Wynn and Berry, my children.

For Joe, my wonderful husband and the funniest man I've ever met,
who encouraged me to write it all down.

TABLE OF CONTENTS

Preface ix

Chapter 1:   Of Funeral Fans and Open Windows . . 1

Chapter 2:   Aunt Daisy and the Silver Dress 5

Chapter 3:   Sunday Visits 8

Chapter 4:   Things I Miss 11

Chapter 5:   Traveling Grandma 14

Chapter 6:   Comparison Is the Thief of Joy 17

Chapter 7:   Are You Old? 20

Chapter 8:   Country Stores 23

Chapter 9:   Farm Living 26

Chapter 10: Porches I Have Known 29

Chapter 11: Kudzu Invades the South 32

Chapter 12: Camping Fun 35

Chapter 13: Eve, Look What You Did! 38

Chapter 14: Fish Tank Stress 41

Chapter 15: Introverts of the World, Blurt! 44

Chapter 16: My Mouth Runneth Over 47

Chapter 17: Routines 50

Chapter 18: The Significance of Senior 53

Chapter 19: School: Yesterday and Today 56

Chapter 20: Relatives I've Known 59

Chapter 21: Another Generation 62

Chapter 22: A Sun-Drenched Elsewhere 65

Chapter 23: Exercises 68

Chapter 24: Avocado and Other Décor Disasters . 71

Chapter 25: Baseball Caps 74

Chapter 26: Christmas Wishes 77

Chapter 27: Down but Not Out 79

Chapter 28: Hunters and Gatherers 82

Chapter 29: Hiding Stuff 85

Chapter 30: I Have Changed 88

Chapter 31: Job Opening 91

Chapter 32: Oops! Moments 94

Chapter 33: Back Then 97

Chapter 34: Our Five Senses 100

Chapter 35: Scars 103

Chapter 36: The Struggle between Body and Mind 106

Chapter 37: Taking Inventory 109

Chapter 38: The Strength of Love 112

Chapter 39: Waiting for Mama 115

Chapter 40: Wanted: Computer Exorcist 140

Chapter 41: What Happened to Sportsmanship? 121

Chapter 42: Why Did We Do It? 124

Chapter 43: Your Joy 127

Acknowledgments 131

About the Author 133

PREFACE

I'm a South Carolina girl.

I grew up on a farm, so I love seeing beautiful fields of crops growing and peach trees blossoming.

I love seeing church parking lots filled on Sunday morning.

I love seeing children outside playing.

I love lakes and rivers and the Atlantic Ocean.

I grew up a half orphan, and my father is one of the first people I want to see when I get to the other side.

Two things that have been my stay all my life are grits and a full bathtub of hot water.

I love pizza, and I eat the leftovers for breakfast when I want to.

CHAPTER 1

Of Funeral Fans and Open Windows

Iremember a time when birds, wasps, and funeral fans were a part of meetings and services at our old Presbyterian church in upstate South Carolina. Windows at the church were massive and always open for services and meetings during the summer— and wasps never missed a service.

Birds sometimes flew in and sailed wildly from one side of the sanctuary to the other. Nervous women could hardly sit still and furiously fanned themselves, not knowing if their hat or dress was a target for bird doo.

As a child, I loved watching the whole scene and was entertained by twisting and contorting in the pew while observing a frantic bird trying to escape church. I knew some frantic adults wanted to do the same.

I especially remember one Sunday during the sermon when a wasp landed on the preacher's collar and crawled all around his neck. Everyone could see it, but he seemed completely unaware. The wasp never stung him. After that, I was convinced he must be God's man—that or the wasp just loved the smell of Argo starch!

At the old church as people came and went, often the floor creaked. During one service, a very large woman stood up to sing the last hymn and promptly fell through the floor. It took several burly farmers to retrieve her and get her to the hospital. She had a broken leg. Little conversation was made of the event, but as a child, I'd always wondered if something like the crash through the floor would happen because of her weight . . . and it did!

On one hot Saturday in June of '49, my best friend, Lou, and I accompanied our mothers to the Women's Auxiliary meeting so we could play on the church grounds that were surrounded by a large historical cemetery dating back to the Civil War era.

The ladies convened in the sanctuary all dressed in hats, girdles, gloves, and hosiery, as was the dress of the day in 1949! Since the church was not air-conditioned, the only moving air came from funeral fans (fans displaying a prominent advertisement for the local funeral parlor), if you were lucky enough to find one stuck in the pew rack.

As we ran the cemetery wall, playing hide-and-seek among

the tombstones, we became thirsty, and so it happened that Lou goaded me to climb through the open window and get some sweet tea and other refreshments.

"Climb in! Hurry up! They could come any minute!" Lou said, as we spotted the refreshment room ripe with mouthwatering morsels. Food was abundant and was always composed of fancy finger sandwiches, canapés, cheese straws, and desserts. No shortcuts were taken because other women *knew* if your food was not made from scratch.

I felt a push, my foot slipped, and down I fell into the ten-gallon galvanized tub holding massive ice chunks and Mason jars of lemonade and tea. Icy water went halfway across the room with hysterical giggles and wet clothes following! Afraid the commotion would bring forth my two old-maid cousins (who never thought anything was funny), we made a hasty retreat and hid behind a huge granite monument of a Civil War soldier.

We saw cousins Iris and Emma arrive to survey the mess; they mistakenly thought a stray dog had done the damage. With no heavenly thoughts about such a dog, they were very vocal about what might happen if the dog came back!

Finally, as we were rounded up to go home, my clothes had dried, and Mama never heard the squish of soggy and water-logged shoes. The "dog incident" was never mentioned.

Recently, I visited the old church. Windows are sealed shut, birds and wasps can only peer in, and sweaters have replaced funeral fans in the now-too-cool sanctuary.

Auxiliary meetings with ladies dressed in hats and gloves and eating homemade refreshments are no more, but young girls still play Hide and Seek in the cemetery and run on the long, rock cemetery wall. Christian fellowship, heartfelt service, and redemption are the better part of the long history of believers who have come from that old house of worship I love and carry in my heart today.

Thankfully, some things never change.

CHAPTER 2

Aunt Daisy and the Silver Dress

Some people just make us smile. And they never seem to wrestle with the ills of the world and are refreshment to our souls when we are longing for laughter. They smile at everyone, and it seems their purpose in life, whether they know it or not, is to gladden hearts.

I had a relative like that. She was slightly zany and was my grandmother's sister. Her name was Daisy, so she signed all correspondence with a hand-drawn daisy flower.

She was a musician and a poet, wore beautiful clothes, was well traveled, had a maid, and lived in town. I first visited her when I was nine. I lived on a farm in Spartanburg County.

Aunt Daisy's life centered on music, and she played and taught piano, cello, violin, and the viola. Her living room was one large conglomerate of instruments all set up in readiness for playing. Being in her living room was an experience unequaled to any others I had had at age nine.

Domestic engineer she was not. Once, when I was thirteen, I ventured to ask what her favorite meal to cook was, and she was aghast and responded, "Oh, my dear child, I don't even know what is in my kitchen; I never go in there!" To a thirteen-year-old farm girl the comment was quite remarkable, and I knew I loved her from that day on.

Once when I was visiting, she suggested we take a ride in her new car . . . a pale purple Cadillac. True to form, she had bought an outfit to match the car: suit, hat, and shoes all the same shade of purple! Unbelievably, she drove to the Department of Motor Vehicles and requested permission for the red South Carolina license tags to be painted purple to match the car. The request was denied.

On another trip, we were traveling on a two-lane road when she decided to go in the opposite direction. Stopping in the middle of the road, she waved to cars coming toward us to stop as she turned her Cadillac around, smiling all the while at the other drivers, who weren't.

Aunt Daisy had musical toilet paper that played as the roll turned, and she also wore musical broaches and delighted in wearing and playing them while watching people look for the origin of the music.

She loved everything beautiful and wrote poetry extolling the beauty of nature, and of the joyful sounds of violins and cellos in symphony. Always impeccably dressed, even when she went to the doctor, she taped paper roses on her derrière so it would be more pleasing to the doctor's eye if she should get an injection. She remarked that her fanny was not her best side, and she knew the sight of the roses would make the doctor smile.

One fall day she took me on an outing, and I commented on her beautiful dress, an elegant, pale-gray, knife-pleated silk dress with a V-neck, wide belt, and three-quarter sleeves with covered buttons. When we arrived back at her home, she told me to stay in the car while she ran into the house.

She reappeared in a different dress but carried the gray dress on a padded satin hanger in a see-through bag. "You should have this dress," she said, "because you are young and it will look much better on you than me." The moment took my breath away. I shall never forget it!

I was sixteen at the time, and she was in her fifties, but the dress was a classic and I had never had such an expensive and exquisite garment. I wore the dress for years and received more compliments on it than any dress I have ever owned, and I felt elegant and self-assured with each wearing. It was just what a shy and unsure girl needed to bridge the gap into young adulthood back in the 1950s.

I loved Aunt Daisy, and the most memorable gift I received growing up came from her.

CHAPTER 3

Sunday Visits

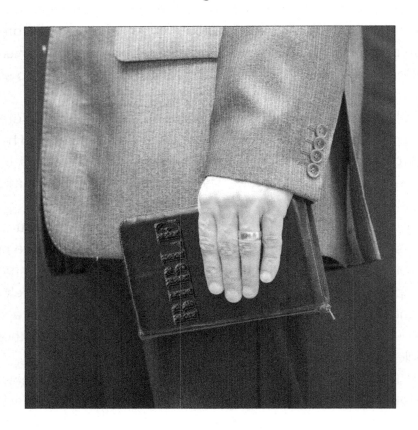

It was a Sunday afternoon and I was ten years old when we recognized the preacher's car in the driveway, and Mama was in her robe because she didn't feel well. It was just one of those days when she was not sick, but just felt tired and thought she might be coming down with something.

Ding Dong goes the doorbell. Mama runs to the bathroom. My twelve-year-old brother disappears, as does my step-father. On her way to the bathroom I hear "entertain the preacher and his wife until I get my clothes on."

My three and four-year-old siblings thought they were the entertainment and so they acted their ages (silly would be an understatement) as I tried to make them behave in front of the preacher and his wife.

There is only so much chatting a kid can do with the preacher, after discussing the pictures on the wall, the weather and school. About fifteen long minutes later, all the while, listening to my mother rub-dub-a dubbing in the bathtub; she glides into the living room as a gracious, smiling Southern lady while emitting the aroma of rose sachet.

How times change. Today, hardly anyone comes visiting before calling first....thankfully. Sundays were the days ministers, neighbors or relatives dropped by. No one called to see if you were at home, they just came. Today with so many women working, and kids playing on different teams there is little time for visits and many people are not at home anyway. We are out grocery shopping, running errands and checking on elderly parents. We use e-mail, Skype and voice mail in lieu of visiting due to time constraints.

When I was growing up we were on a party telephone line with seven other families, so the minister probably couldn't reach us if he tried calling before visiting. The line was always busy.

Another noticeable change about Sundays are our "Sunday clothes", they were separate from other clothes. We had to change into work clothes since the cow had to be milked on Sunday and chickens had to be fed. Such was farm life.

Today most of our clothes are all- purpose for work and

church. And, we women don't have to deal with all the pieces of clothing worn by our mothers and grandmothers such as girdles, hose, petti coats, hats, and gloves. Halleluiah we are free of much of that.

Folks used to say the reason they didn't go to church was that they didn't have anything to wear. That is no longer a valid reason. Today in most church services, people wear blue jeans, Bermuda shorts and sundresses, but some men always wear a suit. I like to think you dress your best for a worship service, whatever your best might be – not clothes that have been lying in the dryer for days. "I'm just saying."

The experience of having to "entertain" the preacher made an impression on me. Unless I am sick or near death, I don't answer my door if I'm not dressed and haven't gotten an e-mail or phone call someone is coming. Some incidences just shape us. I'm sure you have some, too.

CHAPTER 4

Things I Miss

I miss Full Service gas stations from the past. We took them for granted as our gas tanks were filled, oil and water levels checked, windshield washed, and sometimes the back window if there was someone or something interesting back there. (Girls, usually.)

Do you remember Elevator Operators? It was comforting having an operator on board when going to the tenth floor- especially if you are claustrophobic like my best friend. Her dentist was on the ninth floor. She was afraid to ride the elevator up and needed someone with her while walking to the ninth floor. She rode down with her eyes tightly shut while squeezing my arm until we got to the first floor. There was nothing in this world that girl was afraid of or would not do, but she turned into jelly when entering an elevator.

I really miss department stores where sales ladies helped you dress and brought outfits to the dressing room for you to try. And if the garments needed altering, they called the store seamstress and she measured and pinned and told you when to pick up the clothing. We didn't know how to appreciate that service.

Ah! For the lunch counters at Woolworths'. They had great lunch specials and as a child I loved sitting on the bar stool to eat. The waitresses were like well-oiled machines. They made the best BLT's and soup, and they had meat and two veggie plates. When you thanked them for their good service, they always said, "You're welcome" instead of "No problem." (pet peeve showing).

Where is the milkman? There was just something special about hearing the milk bottles placed on the porch. We trusted and loved our milkman, and he knew how to let himself in and put the milk in the fridge if we weren't home.

Now, I'm really going to wax nostalgic. I especially miss the quarterly" Family Night Suppers" or "Dinner on the Grounds" at the Presbyterian Church where I grew up. Not many of us cook the way we used to and we never worried about cholesterol and triglycerides. The women usually made everything from scratch, and the vegetables were from their own gardens or larders. It was an enjoyable time with good fellowship, and the fried chicken was wonderful, fried at home, not bought. (Gone are those days) In the summer months, there was always churned ice cream, and I loved the sound a churn made when the ice cream was ready for the dasher to come out. Peach and Strawberry were the favorites.

I know I am dreaming of a time gone by and have to admit I don't fry chicken anymore and don't "put up" corn, beans, pickles, strawberries, squash, preserves and so on. But, it is always fun to remember what used to be. It was a different time back then, and people didn't feel the need to rush home. No e-mail, Facebook, or Twitter to think about. What will be said forty years from now about what used to be in year 2018?

CHAPTER 5

Traveling Grandma

It is only for one night, but the preparation nowadays for a night away is enough to make the faint-hearted stay home. Years ago, an overnight trip involved throwing a few clothes in an overnight bag with toothpaste and deodorant, and I was off for an adventure. But lo, I am caught unaware of a subtle and unstoppable process that must have begun in the middle of the night about thirty years ago.

As I packed my stuff to visit my five-year-old grandson in Georgia to participate in Grandparents Day, I felt the reality of my age as I gathered all the necessary items for a one-night stay. First, there was medicine for blood pressure, cholesterol, triglycerides, and indigestion. Not bad for starters . . . but I already knew I would need Imodium, and then there was that leaky bladder problem. The arthritis might crop up, so anti-inflammatory tablets were in, as were toe spacers for bunion toes. Thankfully, I can smile and walk at the same time, and wrinkle cream and circle concealer are staples (no need to scare the children!)

What I do not miss from my suitcase of fifty years ago is a girdle (all that tugging and pulling just to get my girth to stay in one place.) Then along came pantyhose, which were great except when they drifted halfway down to my knees. Hooray for thigh-highs and knee-highs, if they stay up. And give me slacks instead of skirts and dresses. My once-youthful legs now look like a road atlas to California, as my doctor told me I was making new veins every day. And that was ten years ago.

When I was a young girl, all my favorite aunts had jiggly arms, which, in my eyes, were a badge of respect, as I observed other adults handling jiggly-armed aunts with kid gloves. It never occurred to me why . . . But now I have jiggly arms, so don't cross me before coffee!

One of the most enjoyable aspects of grandmotherhood is not worrying what people think. There is a certain amount of freedom that goes with age. I am no longer striving to keep up with fashion, and whoever heard of a grandmother with teeth so white they reflect off other people's bifocals? And being retired certainly has the advantage over having to show up at work every day on time, dressed, and in my right mind. Grandmamas do have an unspoken privilege of being a little forgetful and not having all the facts straight every single time we retell a story.

I have great satisfaction knowing I have already been through all the stages in which my adult children are presently engaged: keeping up with other parents, wearing clothes that don't embarrass the children, throwing "wow factor" birthday parties, sports participation, having a school presence, saying "great job" twenty times a day to every child (yours and everybody else's) for just normal behavior, and driving an in-vogue car.

Several years ago, immediately upon deplaning, my three-year-old granddaughter visiting from Florida greeted me with these words, "Oh no! Grandmama, you are wearing boy shoes." My thought is that everyone should wear flat shoes with a big toe box.

My grandson did enjoy my company, since I was able to act silly without fear of looking silly to him. Grandmammas can get away with more than the average person because we are expected to act like, well, grandmamas. He adores it when I pretend to hit imaginary baseballs and run his imaginary bases. We love making up games, and sometimes I win. But I usually allow five-year-old boys to win because losing will come soon enough.

I managed to behave at his school, and I'm sure I will be invited back since my shoes matched, there were no spots on my clothes, my hair was combed, and I acted my age rather than the age of the class.

So, I'm not a traveling-light grandmama, but travel I will.

CHAPTER 6

Comparison Is the Thief of Joy

Teddy Roosevelt once said, "Comparison is the thief of joy." But we don't care; we just keep on comparing our homes, cars, children, spouses, and the way we look. Why?

When will we stop engaging in such a self-defeating behavior? Probably only when we are under the ground. Where has all this comparing gotten us? We are always measuring ourselves to some imaginary ruler in our heads. It is not an accurate measuring device, but that doesn't stop us from using it.

There are all kinds of ways we compare our lives to other

people and find ourselves lacking. I have a good friend who has often confided, "They are so smart, and I feel inadequate because I don't have a degree." She feels less valuable without a college education—but she is one of the most delightful and entertaining people I know. She always speaks to anyone who is not well or struggling in some way. I have often watched her and wished I could be more outgoing like she is. She is just a natural at it and is so valuable to all who know her.

The list of negative comparisons goes on. "They are all so clever and thin and look at me, I'm overweight" is one most of us are familiar with. Then there's the classic "I don't want the group to meet at my house because they all have beautiful homes, and I don't," followed by "They are rich, and we are not; they live on the lake and have a boat." I've heard all these comparison stories this month. Maybe you have used one of those comparisons to denigrate yourself by comparison with friends or relatives. In fact, relatives may be the main group most folks compare themselves to; we really like to talk about them and how they think they are better than us. Of course, the relative being talked about may not have a clue that we feel insecure or are jealous of them.

When I married into a family of seamstresses who talked sewing material like some people talk about food or golf, I made myself feel inferior because I didn't sew. I was never good at it because I didn't like it. But because I was intimidated by all their knowledge of fabrics, I went to a large piece goods store in North Carolina so I could be a part of the "show and tell" that took place every Sunday afternoon when the three sisters-in law and one mother-in law laid out their material and talked about what they were going to make with it. I tried to read up on the subject and make myself into a knowledgeable sewer of fabric.

I was never going to be a good seamstress, and I didn't want to be. My in-laws' skill level and their love of just holding and caressing material reminded me of Julia Child and how she used to pat and knead a cut of meat she was about to cook.

Comparing myself with my new in-laws and their particular gifts was foolish on my part. They didn't expect me to try to be like them; they were just having fun doing what their mother taught them. My mother didn't sew, so I never learned. My mother taught English and creative writing.

NEWSFLASH! There will always be people who are smarter, richer, thinner, and on and on. While we are busy comparing ourselves to others, there is someone who thinks about us the same way. I like being friends with people who are smarter than me and have more money. Sometimes they buy my lunch.

Eleanor Roosevelt said, "No one can make you feel inferior without your consent." My friend shouldn't feel embarrassed because she doesn't have a degree. First, it's nobody's business. And there are many who attended college who should have gone to a technical school instead.

And the tech graduates probably have jobs.

CHAPTER 7

Are You Old?

It was right in the middle of the Sunday school class when she looked up at me with her soulful blue eyes and calmly asked, "Are you old?"

She had watched me many Sundays, but why today? Was it the black dress, or my two days shy of beauty shop day, or the fact I told this five-year-old to put her bottom in the chair instead of feet hanging over the back? Whatever it was, I was not ready to answer totally in the affirmative, but simply said, "I think I must be, since I *am* a grandmama!

Her simple question has made me navel-gaze to myself about

exactly when we become old to five-year-olds. We know we become old to thirteen-year-olds when we reach thirty, but younger children are much kinder in their assertions and are known to humor us even when we are unable to operate a new DVD player.

Are we old when the makeup no longer covers the wrinkles, or is it when our knuckles are gnarled and our scalp shows through our hairdo or when we exaggerate our lips to show we still have them? Could it be when we use words like *record player, phone booth,* or *picture show*, or mumble something about needing a church key?

Children are so perceptive and brutally honest with us adults. No dillydallying around about hair color, skin color, veins, skinny legs, or bad breath . . .

These five-year-olds appear to be in outer space as they listen to a Bible story, twirling barrettes, talking, moving chairs back and forth, fingering anything on the table not nailed down, even playing with the most innocuous sliver of paper until questioned about the story and . . . bingo, they know the answers!

We adults would find ourselves so distracted by wiggling our loose tooth, elbowing our seatmate, tying and retying our shoes, and whispering to no one in particular about our new puppy that we couldn't answer the first question about a story we just heard.

When did we become so inhibited? When did we first think people were staring at us or at least waiting for us to make a mistake?

Somewhere between becoming civilized and reaching our majority, we lose the ability to respond honestly to our fellow humans. The most honest people in the universe must be five-year-olds.

The conversations they have with each other are unique and real. "I have on new shoes . . . My daddy threw up last night . . . Why does your hair look that way today? My brother told a lie this morning . . . She didn't have her eyes closed during the prayer . . . Are you old?" And so it goes.

As adults, we are way too cool to announce our new shoes and don't want people to question us on why Daddy threw up, and we tell other women they look good even if they don't, and we never tell of moral failures unless forced to.

If we could remain like five-year-olds in our human relations, we would all be telling the truth and giving hugs for hurts and making honest assessments regardless of political and social economics.

CHAPTER 8

Country Stores

Grits and Groceries

I sure do miss country stores as I drive through the rural communities in South Carolina and Georgia. Most featured only one gas tank and were rectangular buildings with double doors and a porch on the front. We see remnants of them, but most have fallen down or are barely standing. They used to be the social center of the communities they served, and many were voting precincts where area politicians came to hold stump meetings during election years.

There was one such store across the highway from my home in Spartanburg County.

Mr. Thomas's store served the rural community and carried staple goods, bacon, fatback, bologna, cheese, and canned goods. He sliced the meat and cheese with a huge knife that stayed on the meat counter. I never saw him wash his hands or the knife, but if anyone died from eating meat from his store, we never heard about it.

The store was the school bus stop for about ten of us. On cold mornings, we would all pile inside, huddle around the big potbellied stove in the middle of the store, and wait for the bus. We were extremely noisy; horseplay was always a short minute away from a fight with six roughneck farm boys in the mix. Mr. Thomas pretended to be deaf until an actual fight broke out, and then he ordered everyone outside.

Each day, girls had some boyfriend drama accented by theatrics and much hair combing and lipstick fixing that left a trail of loose hair and lipstick traces on the "ice cream box." He never said a word.

Cotton fields surrounded the store, and in the rural South in the 40s and 50s, local schools let out early when the cotton was ripe for picking. Big croker sack sheets were used to tie up cotton for weighing. Pay was five cents a pound. Many times, when I had picked twenty-five cents' worth, I headed to the store and bought a popsicle, a candy bar, bubble gum, and a Pepsi. We also earned money to spend at the county fair, which always coincided with cotton-picking time.

Once my brother and I decided it would be fun to poke holes in the windows of rice boxes in the storage room. A few days later, with a grave look on his face, Mr. Thomas confronted us. He made us sit down, and at our eye level, he taught us about honesty, responsibility, respect, and forgiveness. It was one of the most life-changing and character-building lessons of my memory. To my knowledge, Mr. Thomas had no religious affiliation, but it was one of the best Sunday school lessons on practical theology I remember.

Mrs. Thomas brought his lunch every day, and the menu never changed. It was fried chicken, rice and gravy, homemade biscuits, and a fresh vegetable from the garden. Mr. and Mrs. Thomas had a ritual that played out every day, too. He would tell her he loved her, and she would get mad and tell him to shut up and eat his lunch. They loved performing this ritual when there was an audience.

The glass candy counter had a long crack right down the middle that Mr. Thomas ignored as he leaned on it daily. Candy was at eye level: Fifth Avenue, Power House, Butter Finger, and BB-Bats. Some days it was too much for young eyes and hearts to stand, so Mr. Thomas paid two cents for every stray drink bottle found in the ditch along the highway. An hour of scrounging area ditches made a five-cent candy bar a delicious prize. Dirty hands and mud-caked fingernails made instant gratification all the more glorious.

I have fond memories of the store and of Mr. and Mrs. Thomas, and they were true friends of my family.

CHAPTER 9

Farm Living

Igrew up on a farm in Spartanburg County. When my stepfather went out of town, sometimes I had to milk Phoebe, the mentally unbalanced cow.

Sometime in Phoebe's past, someone must have hit her in the head with a milk bucket because she clearly had some sort of disorder. Once, when I was going on a date, I found out one hour before the love of my sixteen-year-old life came to pick me up that there was no one else to milk the cow. (Anyone who grew up on a farm can tell you that you can't just not milk a cow.) I had already shampooed my hair and had it in rollers. While I was milking Phoebe, she swished and wrapped her manure-laden tail in my face and hair, and then promptly put her right hoof into the milk bucket. (I said she was disturbed.). Well, I became a drama queen that day about ever milking that cow again.

When you live on a farm, there are animals that must be dealt with on a daily basis. I learned how to be a treetop dweller the year my brother raised an FFA steer. Part of our pasture was in the woods, which used to be my playground, and sometimes the steer treed me. He would lie down underneath the tree and keep staring at me as if just waiting for me to come down so he could obliterate me.

We had hogs, too. I stayed as far away from those animals as possible. I'm surprised I'm not a vegetarian. But I enjoyed my bacon every morning and managed to block out where it came from.

My brother loved to go squirrel hunting, and once when Mama was not home, he asked me to help skin the squirrel and cook it. I am not one bit like Granny from *The Beverly Hillbillies*. That was my first and, I hope, last experience with skinning and cooking a squirrel, although if we had a national disaster, I might have to renege on the comment. One thing is for sure: there are enough squirrels around here to feed many people for a long time.

We always had mules doing most of the hard work of plowing, pulling the hay rake and mowing machine, and hauling the cotton wagons. My favorite farm animal was Red the Mule. He was even-tempered and gentle and the only large animal I was not afraid to be near. If we ever have to go back to the good ole days for transportation, I pick a mule to pull my covered wagon!

People are now beginning to have chickens in their backyards again so they will have fresh, organic eggs. Our chickens were free range in the backyard. I still think the most dangerous animal that chases a child is a rooster. I learned to run fast when entering those birds' sanctuary. In fact, I was a sprinter until high school, when we got rid of those chickens and the attack rooster.

Free range: I love those two words. I was a free-range child and didn't know it. I bet some of you were, too.

CHAPTER 10

Porches I Have Known

L iving in the South all of my life, I have known and loved many porches, especially screened porches. Porches bring the outside in while saving us from mosquitoes, wasps, and rain.

There are porches I have loved for different reasons. My childhood porch is the most memorable, not for its beauty or comfort but for the sanity it brought to my conflicted family. There was always a breeze out there, so we were forced to sit on the porch while the house cooled down in the summertime. Conversations were easier in the dark when faces were obscured by darkness. Being on the porch at night allowed us to be more civil with each other.

Another porch I have known and loved is my aunt and uncle's porch in Spartanburg. Beautiful and well furnished, this one had a soft maroon leather glider with matching chair and a crook-necked lamp. A card table was always up for canasta playing, and there were green drop-down, roll-up shades for privacy. I learned how to play canasta and to take losing with grace, which I am sure I needed.

Another porch I loved was at the summer home of a relative in the Saluda Mountains in North Carolina. It was a wraparound porch with bannisters, several hammocks, and lots of rocking chairs. It looked out over mountain cedars, a low rock wall, mountain laurel, and white gravel. My cousin and I would claim a hammock and take turns swinging each other with childlike abandon. We often stayed out there and watched the mountain fog roll in.

The porch of my childhood best friend was special. It was minimally furnished with two hard rocking chairs painted white and a bench that rocked. The floor was cement, and there were no plants or greenery. We could see all the traffic on the country road that ran in front of the house: cattle trucks, hay balers, and tractors with disc harrows. But what made this porch special was the warm and memorable conversations with my friend's mom, who was my second mother. She was always interested in what was going on in my life.

My last most-favorite porch was the one we had in the Low

Country near the beach. Of course, it was screened to keep away no-see-ums and giant mosquitoes. It had a glass-top table with four cushioned chairs where we ate most of the year. The porch overlooked a large backyard with magnolias, hydrangeas, azaleas, confederate rose, river birch, gardenias, and a fig tree. Every day we experienced the joys of nature while trying to solve the world's problems on that porch. We watched birds and squirrels at the bird feeder. We watched as a cardinal built her nest just inches away from the screen. We were so happy to provide her a place to lay her eggs so close to where we sat and watched. Sadly, we were not out there when a predator stole her eggs.

A good friend painted a five-by-four-foot scene of two parrots in a tree on one back wall. There were two large cushioned rocking chairs. The floor was a brown stained wood, and the ceiling and trim were white. Truly, it was my happy place!

Porches bring the outside in and are memorable and useful as refuges, not only from heat but also for the relationship building that takes place there. Everyone is more at ease, birds can be heard and watched, and sweet iced tea even tastes better on the porch.

CHAPTER 11

Kudzu Invades the South

Ihave been spending some time in my dentist's office in Pendleton, and behind his office is one of the healthiest kudzu patches you'll ever see. If you grew up anywhere from the edge of Texas to Kentucky, I don't have to identify kudzu for you. But someone new to the area might look at this alien green vine and wonder what it is and why it seems to be everywhere.

The vine actually came from Japan and was planted in the southern United States as a means to control erosion. We happen to have the perfect climate for kudzu; it covers seven million acres in the South. In 1902 the plant became known as "the front porch vine" because it made good shade when people sat on their porches. It is said that Sherman couldn't conquer the South, but kudzu has.

Of course, when the first frost comes you will see how very fragile the leaves are. The green vine suddenly becomes brown, and the lush green leaves die until spring comes again. But as sure as night follows day, kudzu will be back year after year because there are no known predators to kudzu.

Most herbicides don't work on kudzu, and some even make it grow faster. It can grow sixty feet in a year. However, Angora goats constantly grazing on kudzu will eventually eradicate it. Over near the golf course on Perimeter Road at Clemson University, six or eight goats have been engaged to do away with (for the time being) this invasive vine that is covering the South.

Kudzu actually belongs to the legume family. Some people deep-fry it, and it's 22 percent protein, so it's good for us, and cows and horses think it is candy! You might wonder, why not bale it up for livestock if it is so good for them? Well, since kudzu was planted to control erosion, much of the vine is in deep ravines and cannot be easily harvested.

Nancy Basket—yes, that is her name—of Walhalla is a nationally known expert on kudzu and a contemporary basket maker and fiber artist whose work is in galleries across the southeast. She makes paper, baskets, and lampshades from kudzu and has been creating kudzu products for twenty-five years. Her kudzu leaf art cards are just beautiful. She says kudzu grows twelve inches a day, and if you sit and watch, you can actually see it grow. I believe that!

Ms. Basket told me we don't need to worry about kudzu taking over our forests and woodlands because it needs sunshine to grow. We usually see it on the edges of woodlands and not in the woods. I'm glad for that information! Roots can weigh up to 440 pounds and are over seven feet long. Some kudzu plants can take ten years to kill. In 1953, the government finally realized kudzu was out of control and recommended stopping the planting of the vine. Duh.

Maybe we just need to have more goat farms. Repeated application of goats seems better than repeated applications of herbicides since they are not effective anyway. Besides, goats are more earth friendly and are fun to watch. Kudzu and goats— made for each other! A good partnership in the South.

CHAPTER 12

Camping Fun

There we were, travel trailer novices parked on the beach in south Florida on spring break. We dreamed of warm weather and fun on the beach, but Mother Nature had another idea. The first day the heavens opened for the entire day. The next morning we awoke to the brightest Florida sun that could possibly shine—but unbelievably it was forty-five degrees with a howling wind. Two eight-year-olds and a nine-month-old baby cooped up in a camper was not the getaway we expected. This cold snap was the worst south Florida had seen in a decade. Bummer.

Meanwhile, my husband very quietly and softly said, "I think I need to see a doctor. Something is wrong with my eyes." (This man never went to a doctor, so I knew it must be bad.) The pain was such that he could barely open his eyes.

Thankfully, we located a medical complex. I had to lead him into the office. We were a sight. The girls pranced around in shorts and flip-flops as if it were July Fourth. The baby was crying. The natives were all wearing coats with hardly any skin showing. There was no hiding the fact that we were tourists.

The diagnosis: iritis, a painful infection in both eyes. The treatment: keep all light away from his eyes (here in the Sunshine State). The medication made him almost immobile. So, here we were in our travel trailer with every shade drawn to keep out light. We'd reserved the camping site weeks ahead since it was a busy tourist time. Believe me, we had the entire beach to ourselves; even the birds left.

I managed to take the disappointed girls to the mall while my husband sat in the travel trailer with his eyes closed. The weather never warmed, and the medical situation had no quick fix. Under the circumstances, we decided we should go home. I quickly learned how to tow a trailer.

We had traveled about fifty miles to gas up, and while waiting, my husband decided to open his power window. It refused to go back up. We were not riding in a jalopy, but power windows in a five-year-old car could be tricky. The girls were cold in their inappropriate clothing. The only thing large enough to cover the window was the baby's blanket. So, we closed the door on the blue blanket to try to keep the wind and the cold out. It flapped wildly in the wind as we made our way. Tacky.

About twenty miles later, we suddenly heard a high-pitched sound like a police car was after us. The faster we went, the louder the noise. We couldn't figure where the obnoxious sound was coming from. But it seemed to have something to do with the speedometer. Who ever heard of a speedometer cable breaking?

Talk about Beverly Hillbillies! There we went, a blue baby blanket covering the window and flapping in the wind and the high-pitched squeal of the speedometer all the way back to South Carolina. My husband was wincing at the pain in his eyes and felt helpless about the whole situation. The girls with too much togetherness in a small space were crabby. The baby's schedule was all upset, and his "blankie" covered the window and he wanted it. In the winds like the Ides of March, the trailer swayed and groaned at the hands of this rookie driver.

"All's well that ends well" and home never looked so good. Camping, anyone?

CHAPTER 13

Eve. Look What You Did!

Eve, just look what you did when you ate the fruit of the tree of knowledge of good and evil.

First, what about all the pain during childbirth? And that pain does not stop there; we have to worry about our offspring until we are laid in the ground. There was no worry before you ate the forbidden fruit.

Look at what our men have to endure. Did you not feel sorry for all those roofers and road crews and landscapers during our 100-degree weather this summer?

The original garden you lived in only needed tending. There were no weeds or pests to deal with there. Now we have cutworms, aphids, slugs, brown rot—and don't get me started on wasps. You never had a wasp fly under your dress at an outside birthday party when you were ten years old. Well, I did, and I showed the world my underwear with my dress pulled up around my neck to get that varmint away and keep it from stinging me anymore.

And you never had the opportunity of driving with your baby in heavy downtown traffic with a mad bumblebee frantically zooming around in the car, not being able to stop and get the bee out of the car. If you hadn't been kicked out of the garden, the bee would have been a nice bee and not interested in stinging. All you had to say was, "Nice bumblebee, go back to your flower, you sweet thing," instead of being hysterically afraid the bee was going to sting your baby.

Another thing you didn't think about on that fateful day of sin and disobedience: you never broke an ankle or even stubbed your toe or had to have impacted wisdom teeth extracted. And you and your Adam never needed a colonoscopy or had the flu or a stomach virus.

You never craved chocolate ice cream or gravy biscuits knowing you shouldn't eat them because of diabetes or heart problems. In fact, you had a perfect body and never got cancer or arthritis or even migraines, and you never got blisters when you tended the Garden. Now see what you have done to all of us? We get old and have diseases and even personality disorders.

Also, Adam was never laid off because his company was

downsizing or closing. He also never had to decide whether to buy groceries or pay the utility bill.

Girl, you blew it for yourself and the rest of us. So what are we going to do? We now know mishaps, accidents, and illnesses are a part of life and are going to happen, period. We know it started eons ago, and the world is broken and can't be fixed by politicians or ourselves. Anyone who doesn't believe that should park his or her new car in a busy parking lot or eat soup with their tie on, or brag on their perfect (NOT!) child to other parents.

Maybe that is why we cling to our childhood beliefs about the world. We just knew when we became adults we would have power over our lives and would win, win, win because we were well-educated and smart. Tsk, tsk. How silly we were.

Basically, Eve, everything is more complicated because of you. How about the following conversation?

"Hello, is this ABC Roadside Service? My car has a flat and I'm on 1-85 in five o'clock traffic. Can you send someone out to change the tire?" "Lady, our computer system is down and we're not sure when we can send someone . . ." Blah, blah, blah. See what I mean?

CHAPTER 14

Fish Tank Stress

Does your doctor's office have a fish tank? Mine does, and those fish seem to be swimming faster and faster these days. If only they could talk! What things they've heard and seen from us humans waiting for appointments.

There was the woman who insisted on clipping her finger-nails into the inner sanctum of her pocketbook. Clip, clip, and more clips echoed in the waiting room we shared. The fish stared mesmerized and trancelike, then raced to the back of the tank! Who knew clippers were so loud and she was so unconscious of how unpleasant this ritual was? How many clipped nails does she carry around in there anyway?

The sign plainly says Turn All Cell Phones Off. But when this older man's phone began loudly playing "The Star-Spangled Banner," I didn't know whether to stand up and put my hand over my heart or point to the sign. Instead, I looked at the fish as they were chasing each other around the coral at breakneck speed.

How many cell phone conversations have the fish been privy to?

Another time, the waiting room was full when a ring tone went off so loudly we thought the fire alarm had sounded.

The phone's owner informed the man she was sitting with, "I'm not going to answer that because she knows you are sick and we are here."

Another bloodcurdling ring pierced the crowd. (I saw a small fish jump straight up out of the water and do the sidestroke.) The woman decided to answer after all.

"Hey, I knew it was you calling. You know your daddy's here to give a specimen."

We all looked in his direction and could feel his embarrassment. "Daddy" never said a word but continually sank lower into the chair.

Can a fish cry?

And do fish care when self-important businessmen want the world to know they have power or money and loudly transact affairs?

"I put $100,000 on that project and I had better get some results."

Heck, we're all just trying to pay the monthly bills. We don't care about your project! Anyway, "Be quiet, you twit; can't you see I'm trying to read the December 2008 *Sports Illustrated*?" (I was hoping for, at least, last year's *Good Housekeeping*.)

"Are you talking to me?" I asked a woman who suddenly started a conversation asking how I was doing. I tried to tell her I was glad she asked, as she was looking at me, but she never let me answer and kept right on talking. Then I got a glimpse of her other ear. A Bluetooth! I'm not sure, but I think one of those fish snickered at me.

"Just keep acting like you like him, even if you don't, so you can get more jewelry," she said to her cell phone partner-in-non-morality training.

One goldfish is now on his back not moving!

The nurse opens the door with a smile and calls my name as I tell her some of the fish need medical attention.

CHAPTER 15

Introverts of the World. Blurt!

know you're out there. You may be in a family surrounded by talkative, energetic blabbers. Those extroverts! The second a thought comes across their brain, it is out their mouth like turning on a faucet. How I envy them as I struggle to mimic their freedom at parties, in meetings, and at work. Oh, to be glib tongued and think fast on our feet just to show them we are clever, too.

If you are an introvert you may feel everyone else is dancing the Texas two-step while you are doing the hokey-pokey. You wish you could think of comebacks or even better, just say something meaningful before the extroverts have said it all.

However, I've noticed that in a group we are very valuable. Because we often have a better answer, just later than our more animated, "idea in the head in one second, and out the mouth" extroverts. Even though we can appear glazed or even zoned out in a group, we are smart and have many skills . . . but, rather than sharing our smarts, we just want to drop them off at the door and go home.

Introverts are outnumbered three to one, so we must jump in and be heard before we get too old to care. How can we do that? For starters, we must learn the art of blurting. People seem to listen when someone blurts. We can practice blurting before we leave home for a party or any gathering or event.

We can blurt something to the first person we see at a party or function. "Hi! My name is Jenny Jump-In and I am so glad to be here, and how do you know the hostess, and could I get you something to drink?" After you realize you were blurting to the hostess, you may be found picking imaginary lint off your clothing near the exit trying to remember if her name tag said Mable, Sable, or Gable as you blurt to a lone man standing nearby. "Good-bye, I need to go check my Facebook page."

Once, I worked at a job where I was constantly told I needed to mingle with people directly related to our business. All I wanted to do in these large social confabs was hold up a back wall and use the restroom a lot. To flit around the room and mingle made me feel like the proverbial cat in a roomful of rocking chairs.

But I am improving; I have learned a new art of interrupting. Here's how it works: As the extroverts are expounding, just start talking while they are still talking. Eventually they will stop when they realize you are not! This may not win many friends at first, but just jump in to get your point across anyway . . . you may never get this opportunity again. (Kinda like on Fox News). If you repeat this scenario often, you will gain confidence and no longer need to interrupt.

After all, you have waited patiently for years to be a part of conversations, only to have the topic changed while you are waiting your turn to speak. So empower yourself and just blurt!

CHAPTER 16

My Mouth Runneth Over

How often we have this problem. We are talking, and we don't know when to stop, and so we keep going and later wonder why we didn't stop when the stopping was good. Even good speakers have a tough time stopping when they are on a roll talking about their subject. It's smart to leave people wanting to know more rather than them saying the talk was five minutes too long.

Sometimes the way the conversation is going can add to our problem with Too Much Information (TMI.) How can we tell when we are talking too much? Well, do you get interrupted a lot? Can you recognize when there is a glazed look on the faces of the folks you are talking to? Are people shifting in their seats, looking at their watches/devices, or looking away as you are talking to them?

Did you ever get home from a meeting or just being with a group of people and start thinking over some of the conversation and wondering why you didn't bite your tongue when a certain subject was broached? You jumped in and had your say, but then you worried you said too much and promised yourself that next time you were going to be more careful about giving your opinion on whatever was being talked about.

Why do we continue to do this when we know better? Sometimes we are having such a good day that we get full of ourselves and want to give the benefit of our vast experiences and knowledge on a subject to our hearers, so they can be as educated as us!

Beware of the quiet ones when you are in a group. For example, the conversation turns to children: childhood illnesses, potty training, temper tantrums, and other problems with rearing children. You start giving advice in these areas while the entire time, a person sitting quietly across the table just watches you with a look you can't quite figure out. Later you find out she is a pediatrician. She never said a word, and you hope you never, ever see her again as long as you live. Your mouth ranneth over.

Be careful also when you start dropping or calling names. It may come back to bite you. Even if you are discussing (gossiping about) a family that lives one hundred miles away, someone may be a relative or a good friend of that family. Remember, this is the South. I am amazed so many of us are related.

Sometimes we excuse ourselves when our mouth runneth

over by saying, "Well, somebody needed to say something, so I just said it." We don't always know if the message changed the behavior of the person we were aiming at or if it went right over the head of the intended person. Was it said out of concern for someone's safety? Was it said without malice? If we are used to telling people what to do because we are in occupations where advising is part of our job description, then it is easier for our mouth to runneth over because it is required in the work world. Sometimes changing gears may be hard for us when we are away from work.

How do we control ourselves when we think we have solutions to someone's problem or we have an opinion on a subject we think people need to hear? There are three questions we need to ask ourselves before our mouth runneth over:

Is it necessary?

Is it true?

Is it kind?

Those answers should guide us when we are deciding whether to speak up. They'll keep us out of a lot of trouble.

People are more sensitive these days about speech except on social media, which is like the Wild West, where it seems nothing is sacred.

CHAPTER 17

Routines

We all have routines, things we do regularly and always the same way. Good thing, too. Example: we always had fried chicken for Sunday dinner when I was growing up. We could depend on it. But some of our routines change with age and time, so you may have some routines nowadays you never had before, particularly when it comes to buying stuff at a grocery store or drug store.

Routines give us parameters that enable us to get things done. But now a routine as simple as buying toothpaste has changed.

It's not simple anymore. I wish the toothpaste makers would stop. Don't we have enough brands? Each brand has unique features: gentle whitening, extra whitening, multibenefit, bright and strong, extra fresh, extreme whitening, mint, etc. Enough already!

All kinds of routines in the grocery store have changed because of marketing tactics. I used to run in and pick up a loaf of bread. The bread would be at the end of an aisle; now half of the aisle is all about bread! Would you believe thirty-four different ways you can have your bread? There goes that routine if someone else has to go to the store for you. What about power seed bread or good seed bread or sweet Hawaiian bread? No one can pick up your bread for you because how will they know what bread to get?

Years back we had Ivory soap, and if your hands were really dirty, there was Lava or Octagon. (Did your mother ever wash your mouth out with soap? That was a routine exercise my mother provided if I said a cussword. I stopped liking Ivory soap because of that experience.) But yesterday when I went to pick up some soap—oops, sorry, "body wash"—I realized it is not a routine now when we just want to buy soap. Now there are soaps that moisturize, pamper, hydrate, nourish, and cleanse (really!).

Plus, now I have to decide between hair and body wash together, and if I want to smell like my deceased hubby I can buy Old Spice Body Wash. There are so many choices of Old Spice it makes my head spin—fifteen fragrances! So, there are contingencies connected to soap buying each time. Men have to be confused about how they want to smell and for how long. Then again, I'll bet most of the buying of men's body wash is done by women.

I used to love Cheez-Its and may have sent a child into the store to get a box. There are now thirteen different kind of Cheez-its. Another ritual bites the dust.

A friend of mine suggested a solution for some of these problems: we can go back to our past routines of baking our own bread of choice and brushing our teeth with baking soda, like I did as a child when we ran out of Colgate. We could all save money and time by heeding that good advice, and the aroma of home-baked bread is a routine that I could get used to again.

CHAPTER 18

The Significance of Senior

Oh, how my classmates and I looked forward to being a senior in high school, a senior in college, senior vice-president of something, anything, or the oldest on the team. Wow! Senior member of a firm, senior pastor, senior military manager, senior *everything* sounds great until the day we, meaning those of us of a "certain age," start receiving information from AARP. We are taken aback when we first realize we're on their mailing list. "What! I'm not ready for this. They have their nerve. I'm only fifty!" most of us think to ourselves. Sorry, newly designated old-timer. This is only the beginning.

The process really picks up steam when we look at the menu in a restaurant and realize there's a different menu for seniors. We tell ourselves, *Hmm, well, maybe this one time I will take advantage of this discount. Just this one time.* Fast food restaurants start giving us free drinks. And if someone lives to be eighty-five, he or she can get a "big" discount on certain products. Whoopee, a five-cent saving on my hamburger if I make it to eighty-five!

Something happened between being the senior member of a staff and whatever else we were senior of to becoming a Senior Citizen. Suddenly the title "senior" means little. The prestige is gone. What's happening here? How did we slip from significance to insignificance? At this point in our lives, we should be the leaders of our countries. We strove all our lives to be senior of something, but alas, after achieving distinction in the business world, there's nowhere else to go. How can we change such a misguided manner of thinking? In many Asian countries, age is respected and revered. Why are older folks treated so negligently in the United States? What are we to do?

If we decide to kick up our heels and have some fun by taking all kinds of lessons, our children and our neighbors think we're getting Alzheimer's or worse. After all, they can no longer say it's the middle-age crazies because now we're over fifty. Everyone knows the signs of the crazies; men in their late forties start wearing unbuttoned shirts—the better to display their chest hair--buying convertibles and wearing neck chains. Women start trying to look like their daughters. Some wear clothing much too young and short for anyone over twenty-five. They may buy toe rings and ankle bracelets or start wearing lots of glittery, sparkly stuff. We don't like gray hair, so if our hair was brown or black "back in the day," those of us who were former brunettes start sporting various shades of blond or whatever else comes out of the bottle of hair dye. What happened to the blue hair we used to joke about? Somehow, it's no longer funny. But hey, we do have blue fingernail polish now. (I've heard doctors can diagnose certain diseases by the color of our nail beds. Sorry, Doc.)

Those of us who are senior citizens have been through a lot: marriage, toddlers, teenagers, grief from broken marriages, buried parents or spouses, and job losses, and all the other misfortunes and challenges that make up a life. By the way, whoever came up with the term "right-sizing" never lost his/her job or he would know the word is folderol to victims of the phenomenon.

But here we old folks are, some of us still working forty hours a week, the rest either working part-time or volunteering while working crossword puzzles, taking classes, gardening, becoming more adept with the internet, and trying to work these confounded phones so we can get ahead of Alzheimer's. We should be proud of our gray hairs and wrinkles because they are battle scars, badges of honor, tangible proofs of our strength and resiliency. So, do not minimize us because we are Senior Strong!

CHAPTER 19

School: Yesterday and Today

Oh, phooey! Summer vacation is over. But hooray! School is back in, so watch out for school buses. School is so different now, and after touring my old high school recently, seeing blackboards gone and all the technology added, I don't think I could make the grade. The highest form of technology in my generation was running the mimeograph machine and the film projector. The film always broke, teachers hated it, and students loved it because it took up class time taping the film back together.

In the third grade, my teacher went row by row each Monday morning asking if we had gone to church on Sunday. I remember going some Sundays when I wanted to stay in bed but feared being counted among the ones in class who skipped church. She always asked *why* we didn't go . . . that's the part I dreaded. How times have changed.

Fourth grade was too serious, and I decided to make some humor. My Pop Pop showed me how to take a small jewelry box, cut a hole in the bottom, dip my middle finger in ink, stick my finger through the hole, and put cotton all around it. He said to ask people if they wanted to see my cousin's "finger" that had been cut off. (I hope my grandchildren don't read this.) I was quite popular for a while until somebody said I should show it to a certain teacher.

She could hardly believe what she was seeing and started screaming. When she screamed, I got scared and partially moved the finger to show her it was really my finger. She almost fainted. It was fun while it lasted. Today almost anyone can Photoshop a picture of such a finger. But how much fun is that?

My fifth-grade class was next door to the principal's office, and there was an echo as we heard boys being paddled every day with a homemade paddle with three holes. Whenever that activity was in progress, we never heard a word the teacher was saying—we were all counting the licks. Some boys never made a sound, but others added drama by yelling "Ow! Ow!" with every lick.

In the seventh grade, we had a devotional each morning. After the Bible reading, we all had to quote a Bible verse. Sadly, we overworked John 11:35 ("Jesus wept").

In the eighth grade, we had an English teacher who daily broke number-two pencils in half. It all had to do with bad boys in the back of the room trying her patience just to see how many pencils they could make her break.

In the tenth grade, we had a boy who could throw his voice. He made a high-pitched whine, usually in the middle of the class period. Mrs. Jones walked the aisles up and down trying to find the culprit. She never did. It was smiling Don, who smiled at her and chewed gum all the while, making the obnoxious sound.

Now we have a problem that was nonexistent when I was in school. With the advent of all the electronics, people don't need to talk to communicate—they just send a text. Do we need to start classes on how to talk to each other? Look around and watch. Nobody is talking, but their fingers are.

So teachers, watch out! Your students can text you to say, "The dog ate my homework," or "It was on my flash drive, and I put it in my pocket; there was a hole in my pocket and it fell out," or "I e-mailed the homework to you. You didn't get it? Well, I sent it."

Oh, for the good ole days. Bless you, teachers.

CHAPTER 20

Relatives I've Known

The old saying "We can pick our friends, but we can't pick our relatives" is oh so true. We invite them to family gatherings and weddings. They always show up at funerals and we are silently wondering what they might do or say to friends who were unaware you have a relative with few social filters. Of course, these are the relatives who are eager to meet your friends and may blurt out random information to them such as: "She's older than me, but I taught her everything she knows. "

In my family, the female relatives are more colorful than the men. An example is a cousin of mine whose husband is a long distance truck driver and he persuaded her to get her license to drive with him. She is hardly five feet tall, and I don't know how she gets up in the cab of the truck, much less drive the rig. But she did get her license.

They were traveling somewhere on the interstate and he was asleep in the sleeper part of the truck and she was driving. She was listening to music and probably singing along when he popped his head out and said, "Cora, something is wrong with the truck. Don't you hear that noise?" She said," I don't hear anything. He lay back down in the sleeper, but quickly poked his head out again." I'm going to look out the window and try to see what is making that noise." He looked. "Quick get off the road, we are dragging something under the truck. Pull over as soon as you can."

Well, they were dragging something all right – a small car, caught between the front and back wheels of the trailer. The man was unhurt, but very frightened and said," I just knew I was going to die." He had soiled his clothes, but was unhurt.

This happened when Cora moved from the passing lane to the right lane and somehow did not see the car. She was charged with an illegal lane change.

Another relative who was working on her Thanksgiving dinner last year when she became too hot cooking fried okra. She is known to get into the" Ripple" during holidays. She had been cooking and "nipping", so her judgement was not what it should have been. She just knew she was hot and remembered she had two ice pouches in the freezer; so she placed them in her shirt (use your imagination here because I am trying to be delicate) and kept on cooking until she realized they had melted and she needed to remove them. Uh Oh! She had turned two parts of her anatomy black and she was in pain. She was very frightened and drove to the nearest Urgent Care. The doctor trying to keep a straight face said, "I have never seen anything like this." He burst out laughing. She didn't think it was funny and got mad at him for laughing. He prescribed some pain relief. In the end, every-thing turned out all right, but lesson learned:" There are just some places ice packs should never go".

I have more relative stories, but these two are the wildest, and are true. One fun thing to do is to tell your funny stories at family gatherings, as long as the stories are not hurtful. Both of these relatives have related these stories. They enjoy telling them, and each time and we laugh because they are so funny. Humor at family confabs is important and keeps everything light hearted and everybody goes home happy. (Well, most of the time.)

CHAPTER 21

Another Generation

When we were young and newly graduated from high school, we thought we had the world by its tail. There were class prophecies and superlatives and athletes with big dreams and academics who planned to set the world on fire with their intellect. Everyone had ideas about how the world could change when they were in charge.

We looked at our families, and if we were honest, we were already saying how we would do life differently when we were married, how we would never put up with bad bosses and jobs that don't pay what we're worth, and we would never stay in a dead-end job.

We said we would never lose our figure or physique—we would never get fat! We would never live in certain neighborhoods, never drive an old car or buy clothes at Walmart. After all, we had heard it said so much in the media that we deserved certain things, so we wouldn't settle for less than we were worth. People on television looked so happy when they bought certain products, and we deserved to be happy, not like our parents, who were always scraping to get by. We were tired of that.

So, we were off to college or tech school, all about getting ahead and preparing for what we were not quite sure. The girls checked out all the guys (well, not all of them, not the ones who were driving old geeky cars and wearing uncool clothes. The guys checked out all the good-looking girls and dreamed about how to make a good impression on one or any.

We had one problem, and that was deciding what our needs were. We knew all our wants, and didn't those just kind of mesh in with our needs? We needed to appear cool and have our hair in the latest style and use the right gel.

We were young and fresh and energetic. How could we fail? We knew all the hit songs and movies friends raved about.

Some of our long-held beliefs were tested; the morals our parents taught us didn't always fit in with the lifestyles around us, as we were away from home and among strangers. Our instructors were not like our high school teachers. They just told us what they expected and left it up to us to figure it out the rest for the semester.

We found out our families were not perfect, but we wondered how some people could walk around looking sane after they told us some awful stories about their families. We ended up rethinking our idealistic versions of what we thought our lives would be like. We discovered the best-paying and most-fulfilling jobs could get boring and tedious. Raking and scraping were not so bad when we were working toward a goal, and we grew appreciative of such experiences in our background. That knowledge helped us as we found out how much better it is to drive an old car than to be saddled with car payments for the new one, just to be *in fashion.*

Life changed us as we became a part of the real world of working, raising a family, and dealing with losses that come and are a part of life. We quickly learned the difference between our wants and our needs. We got over our foundation being shaken in our college days and are surprised we look a whole lot like Mama and Daddy.

CHAPTER 22

A Sun-Drenched Elsewhere

A sun-drenched elsewhere is where my mind goes when I'm dreaming, when I need a break from my day-to-day life. It usually happens when I become overwhelmed with work, family situations or the weather. The desire usually comes more often in the wintertime as we get tired of cold and rainy weather. (I'm there right now.)

Where is that place for you? A sundrenched elsewhere often involves more than the view. We all dream of these places, but experiencing them is a different matter altogether. Do we look for such places when we are discouraged about our lives, or when we have more bills than paychecks?

This need is different from a bucket list; we may have been working on our bucket list for years. We didn't know what to call it when we dreamed out loud and said to ourselves, "One of these days I'm going to leave this town and go be a cowboy in Texas," or "I'm going sell this house and travel the United States in a Winnebago." Or move to Australia. Whatever. Well, the lawyer never went to Texas, the friend did sell his home and traveled the country, but my brother never moved to Australia. Bucket lists usually cost money, though. Which reminds me that I started out with nothing and I still have most of it. So, a bucket list becomes a "chuckle bucket." We must have one so when people ask what is in our bucket we can chuckle because we don't remember, and we might make up stories or change the subject. We can always say, "What's in my bucket is a secret." Only my closest friends know, and my secrets are safe with them because they can't remember them either.

But unlike a bucket list, oftentimes our sun-drenched elsewhere comes upon us suddenly, when we aren't looking. Little things can take us there. For example, this morning during exercise class, our wellness coordinator played fifties music, and immediately I was transported back to high school, and it sure felt like a sun-drenched elsewhere. I was young again and remembered carefree and uncomplicated happy times associated with life and music in the fifties. It lasted for only for a few minutes, but it was remarkable how quickly the music from years ago brought forth images and feelings of yesteryear that are stored in my memory bank. For a magical moment, I was once again that girl who had the world by its tail with dreams and aspirations, not fears and apprehensions. I loved it.

My sense of smell can also transport me back to a different time or experience. The sense of smell is the strongest of our senses. We can get along without that sense and do all right, but personally I wouldn't want to be without it. I wouldn't know if I was smelling brownies or green beans cooking.

When I was growing up there was a lilac bush near my bedroom window, and I remember the smell of lilac blooms. Anytime I get a whiff of that fragrant bush, I imagine myself sitting at that bedroom window.

When I get a whiff of a man wearing of Old Spice cologne, I think my husband has come back from his grave. So far I have restrained myself from hugging some unsuspecting man because he smells of Old Spice. But I am reminded of my sun-drenched elsewhere when I smell that fragrance.

I am sure in July I will not be dreaming of a sun-drenched elsewhere unless it is connected with air-conditioning. But in the meantime, happy dreaming.

CHAPTER 23

Exercises

What kind of exercise is your favorite, or which ones do you do best? Of course, we know walking, swimming, and bicycling are all very good.

But some exercises cause us to get into trouble with friends, neighbors, and family, exercises like *flying off the handle*. As we age we should know better than to do that knee-jerk exercise because it usually calls for an apology afterward.

We are getting too old for this next exercise, too, but we keep pushing our luck. How many times a week do you exercise this way? It's called *jumping to a conclusion.* Oh, how easy that one is when we don't have all the facts about a situation. We put our own spin on the circumstances and then we *rush to judgement,* which is another favorite exercise.

Charging ahead is yet another way we exercise our brilliance when we get impatient with circumstances and think we need to take things into our own hands so something will get done. We act too quickly without thought or planning. Oi, guilty!

The easy exercise of *assuming:* we do that because we think we have lived long enough and are experienced enough to safely act on what we believe are the correct assumptions. But a situation is never exactly what we assume. Even so, it remains a favorite exercise for many of us. We should never assume anything: there are too many extenuating circumstances. The solution is to simply ask questions until we have all the facts about a situation.

Getting into a tizzy — I actually did one of those time-wasting, worrisome, and unnecessary exercises yesterday afternoon. I was gone from home for four hours and left the garage door open enough for my cat, George, to come and go while I was gone. He stays close to home, so when he was still not home after five hours, I *jumped to the conclusion* that the foxes we've been seeing had taken him off. I had already started thinking what I was going to do with his "stuff" and how much I was going to miss him. Then he came home.

Taking the easy way out is another exercise that defines us when we don't want to get involved. We say we don't have time or we don't want to defend somebody for fear we might look bad, even though it will help a situation if we did get involved. Think politics, for example.

Another wimpy exercise is *passing the buck.* We shift the blame from ourselves to others. The problem is, blaming others takes more exercise than admitting we messed up. Adam blamed Eve for his disobedience, we blame the government for our problems, and so on. We make someone else responsible for a problem we should deal with. We need to simply step up when we mess up; after all, *making excuses,* a variation on *passing the buck*, burns zero calories, so it's not really worth the effort.

What about *burning our bridges*? What goes up must come down, and when we are on our way up, we'd better be aware of how we got there. Coming back down, we will see those same people who helped us to the top. So don't delete your old friends from your address book. Don't burn bridges you might need to cross again.

Let's try these exercises instead. Lifting someone's spirits. Helping someone carry a burden. Walking a mile in someone else's shoes. Extending a hand to a person who needs a bright spot in his or her day.

Those are good exercises to try. Today is a good day to start. So, exercise away!

CHAPTER 24

Avocado and Other Décor Disasters

R emember when our appliances were "upgraded" from white to avocado? Who in the world thought that would fly? But like sheep we stepped right up and had avocado everything: refrigerators, stoves, and sinks.

Didn't it go well with our shag carpet? My husband and I had shag carpet in the first apartment where we lived. I thought it was great until I stepped on an unseen needle hiding in the carpet.

Whoever invented shag carpet was not a sewer of fabrics. Did you ever lose a needle, pin, staple, or a contact lens in shag carpet? Gone forever—or found by accident.

How about those pink-and-green bathrooms from the fifties? Pink sink, pink tub, and pink toilet—with avocado tile on the wall. Let all that register for a moment. I remember one new minister's wife got sick the first time she went into the bathroom of the house where they were to live and saw with that atrocious color scheme. The appliances in the fifties also came in Petal Pink and Cadet Blue. Hindsight is 20/20, but I still don't know what caused us to love shag carpet, pink bathtubs, and avocado green appliances. Maybe it was temporary decorative insanity.

The 1960s period continued the avocado-colored appliances and gave us hippies, "flower power," and the smiley face, and unfortunately Viet Nam. But it was the decade of change and choice, so in the eighties we also had what I like to call Coppertone appliances. Maybe we had seen too many of the Coppertone suntan commercials, and we imagined ourselves looking like the models. Those girls were beautiful, and we were all in for resembling those suntanned models, too. Yeah, right.

Well, the Coppertone went the way of the avocado appliances. But we still had dark wood-paneled walls. I grew up with a knotty pine kitchen and a red tile floor. As a child, I thought it was awful. I tried to get my mother to whitewash the knotty pine to make it lighter but to no avail. Some people like dark rooms, I guess. We also had a cedar table that looked a lot like knotty pine. The incandescent light did little good on dark, rainy days. To make matters worse, kitchens were always on the back side of the house where there was hardly any light. This is actually depressing me to write about it. Thank goodness, we now we have skylights and fluorescent lighting if our kitchens are on the dark side of the house.

However, I'm sure frontier women who had to cook over a fireplace or on a wood stove would have gladly settled for an avocado appliance. In those days, kitchens were simple spaces with shelf space, a fireplace or wood stove, and a table and some chairs. In the eighteenth century, people trained dogs as Turnspit dogs. Think of the dogs the way hamsters spin on their wheel. There was a round wheel above the fireplace, and a dog was trained to spin the wheel to turn the spit for roasted meats. I just hope those hardworking dogs got to eat some of the meat as payment.

Now we have refrigerators that tell our phones we're out of milk. And our tablets monitor our recipes and food intake. That's taking it a bit too far for me. I don't need a smarty pants tablet to tell me how much food I've eaten. That's none of my tablet's business!

CHAPTER 25

Baseball Caps

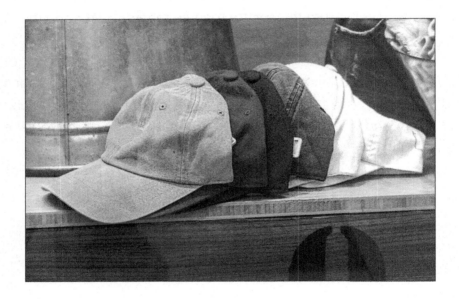

I have a love affair with baseball caps. It really started in junior high (doesn't everything . . .?) My Pop Pop was from "up north" and brought me exotic shoes from time to time (all I know is, the shoes from Ohio didn't look like any from Sears Roebuck in the upstate of South Carolina). He also sent me prairie dresses, but one time he brought me a baseball cap. It didn't seem to go with the full scalloped frocks he brought, but we never hurt his feelings about his gifts. So, at first, I only wore the baseball cap at home. But soon I dared to wear my cap to school.

Who knew a girl in 1952 riding the school bus proudly wearing a Cincinnati Reds baseball cap could cause trouble? I should have. Never underestimate a tomboy going after big bully boys who were throwing her prized possession from front to back of the bus again and again. The driver threatened to stop the bus if the melee didn't end. (In 1952, the bus driver could put a student off the bus for unruly behavior.)

Eventually the boys lost interest in my cap, and I wore it to school the rest of the year, along with the exotic shoes and prairie dresses that looked much like costuming from an Egyptian movie. The shoes were black velvet with thick crepe soles and tied with long velvet crisscross laces halfway up my legs. Other shoes he brought me were sparkly gold ones that always caused comments. But the shoes and the baseball cap together set me apart. What a fashion statement!

None of my friends were interested in baseball caps and continually asked me why I wore one. "Why do you wear that thing to school?" Mary asked as Becky, the class beauty, announced, "You look just like a boy."

"Well, I don't care. I'm going to wear it forever if I want to," I responded defiantly. Who knew I could predict the future?

I think about that conversation when I slip on the bright pink ball cap from Walmart, the one with layers of mosquito spray, and I remember it when I am overdue at the beauty shop and my bedhead hair parts at my crown. On trips to the grocery store, I wear the khaki one with the short bill I bought from an upscale women's store. But I especially like the pale pink one I bought at a sporting goods store that says "Life is good," and it does go well with my bathing suit.

Can a girl have too many ball caps? No way! And I'm still looking for one that would be acceptable for church meetings.

If my Pop Pop from Ohio had not brought me a baseball cap from up north, I would never have experienced a true love affair with a piece of clothing. Some women say they look terrible in a ball cap. I don't believe it . . . Just put one on and fall in love.

CHAPTER 26

Christmas Wishes

I wish there were a mother and a father in every home where there are children.

I wish there were no school dropouts, so everyone could have a fair chance at a good job.

I wish marriage still always came before babies. There are reasons that works better than babies first.

I wish anti-rudeness classes were required in every school, every year, beginning with kindergarten.

I wish girls would refrain from tattoos on their arms, necks, and faces.

I wish people would talk to each other more and text each other less.

I wish I would never, ever again hear the F word come out of anyone's mouth.

I wish people could forgive each other more since we will all need to be forgiven for our failures, too, at some point.

I wish drivers were more patient and wouldn't change lanes constantly and dangerously.

I wish we watched our weight and exercised more.

I wish we had more internal medicine doctors in the surrounding area.

I wish people wouldn't talk during movies, plays, and music presentations. We pay to hear performers on stage, not in the audience.

I wish politicians of both parties would remember why and by whom they were elected and do the work they promised to do when they were running for office.

I wish people would be kinder to all animals, remembering that God loves all His creation.

I wish more of us loved each other despite our differences. As human beings, we really are more alike than we are different, and anyway, when each of us is on his or her deathbed, all that will matter will be whom we loved and who loved us.

I wish for a merry Christmas for all of us, one full of family togetherness, mended relationships, happy memories shared, and, of course, good food.

I wish we would all remember the reason for the season—the birth of Jesus.

Even after two thousand years, wise men still seek Him.

CHAPTER 27

Down but Not Out

We may be down for the count, but don't count us out until we don't come up again! I'm talking about those of us to whom the doctor has said, "It's not going to be long now. They may last a week." Of course, I'm talking about death. But what about three years?

A friend was relating a funny story to me recently about a ninety-eight-year-old relative who had been diagnosed as having only days to live. This relative's caregiver started giving things away, planning for the few days left, and getting her relative into hospice. She went through the patient's clothes and donated them all to a charity.

After about a week, the patient started getting better and kept on getting better. In fact, she was up and about and wanted to wear her regular clothes instead of her bed clothes. She asked her caregiver to go back to her house and get certain outfits. Well . . . uh . . . OK.

The caregiver went down to the charity where she had donated the clothes and had to buy them back. Some had been bought, but she was able to find several outfits still there. That was three years ago! This lady who "only had a few days" is now 101 years old and still going; it seems she got a new lease on life. It was a miracle.

We have heard of people diagnosed with a terminal disease, but then they must leave hospice because they just keep living and are no longer considered terminally ill. We read stories of patients who are not supposed to live who seemingly "defy the odds" and surprise their doctors and relatives by their resilience. Some people just have a fighting spirit and continue in spite of their illnesses. I love stories like that.

So many factors enter into survival in times of illness, and it's an inexact science to try to predict when someone will die. People hang on to life for a special event like a graduation, anniversary, a family celebration, or some private milestone. But it is certainly wise to be prepared with your affairs in order and relationships repaired if you are told you only have a few months to live.

It is also a good idea to have your affairs in order even if you are in good health and only forty years old. Does someone know your passwords, your insurance contacts, your bank account information, your social security number, and the names of people to contact? Do you have a will? Let someone know where it is.

My father was thirty-five years old when he was killed in a car crash. He was too busy with business and "was going to get a will done" when things slowed down. When someone dies without a will, it creates problems for the survivors. Today you can get a will done online, and it is very affordable and legal. So don't wait. You owe it to your family.

It may be later than you think. But don't worry about it. Things happen when they happen. Just make sure nobody gives your clothes away until you are actually gone!

CHAPTER 28

Hunters and Gatherers

Humans started out as hunters and gatherers, and many of us are still hunters and gatherers. In my case, I hunt for my glasses, my phone, my keys, my appointment cards for doctors and dentists, my flashlights, and pens and pencils with ink or points. The number of steps I take in the process of hunting for items I've misplaced is ridiculous, but they do help my Fitbit totals for each day.

I needed to paint a doorframe my son-in-law installed. I had paint—although it was old and needed a lot of stirring—and a drop cloth. I just knew I had a paintbrush, too, but when I got the drop cloth and was ready to paint, some gremlin or other phantom had taken my paintbrush. I hunted in every nook and cranny to no avail, so I made a trip to my hunting-and-gathering place, Ace Hardware.

Last week I got tired of not having enough drugstore glasses because I was tired of always hunting for the ones I had. Off I went to the store to gather a couple more pairs to have around the house. When I entered the store, I realized I had left both pairs of glasses at home. I had to put on a pair off the rack to see if they were the right strength, but I didn't look in the small mirror on the rack to see how the new glasses looked on me.

When I went to pay for my purchase, the cashier looked at me strangely, and there's no telling what she thought when I said, "I need two pairs so I won't be hunting for the ones I already have." I headed out the door, and when I got in my car, I understood what I had done and why the cashier had given me strange looks. I hadn't left both pairs of glasses at home after all. Instead, I had gone to the store and bought glasses with a pair hanging from the front of my shirt and another pair on my head.

What else are we hunting and gathering? It depends on what kind of consumers we are. If we are savers, we are on the hunt for bargains. If we are spenders, we are on the hunt to gather more stuff. Back in the twentieth century, when I was a young woman, some of my friends would occasionally show me what was in their "hope chests," the chests in which young women kept items they would need in their married lives. I didn't have one and always wondered if my friends were actually going to enjoy the contents of the chests when their romantic dreams came true. Some had gathered gowns, china, decorative items, and linens. Would some of these things have the look of yesterday and be dated? Others had quilts their grandmothers had made, and those will never go out of style.

How could we know that society would change so much and so quickly? We thought what we had in our hope chests would continue to be relevant. Some of it was and is, but if I were helping a modern bride find something useful for her chest, I would go for a well-stocked toolbox with a how-to book for repairing everything in the house that breaks. She will use those tools more often than she can realize.

At the end of our lives what will happen to what we have gathered? It depends on what we have loved. The things we gathered may not be what the following generation will cherish. Have you tried to pass down treasures like sterling silver, fine china, and crystal to your children? Those items meant a lot to yesterday's generations, but your children and grandchildren might not be interested in anything that requires polishing and can't be put in a dishwasher. After all, nostalgia isn't what it used to be.

CHAPTER 29
Hiding Stuff

Some people just make us laugh. It's not only what they say but how they say it. I enjoyed an experience last week in a waiting room with one of the funniest women you can imagine. She was telling stories about how she keeps snacks and other sweet treats away from her husband. It seems he has such a sweet tooth that she can't keep goodies for grandchildren or other guests where he can find them. She must ration them out. She even has a lock on her freezer door, so he can't get to the goodies to eat them up.

The marriage has worked for over fifty years, so he must not mind having this arrangement. Every so often, she must find a new hiding place for the key to the freezer. He finds it from time to time, so she has become quite creative in hiding it. I would tell you her current hiding place because it is hysterical, but he (the Sugar Monster) may read this column. And after fifty-plus years of hiding the freezer key, there aren't many places left in the house for her to use.

I bet some of you have hidden goodies to keep them safe for celebrations or from your toddlers or teens. My mother used to hide lemons in her underwear drawer because my brother and I ate lemons. She often made lemonade, and she got tired of not having enough lemons. The only way I found where she hid them was when she asked me to get a gift for someone out of her drawer and I found out she hid everything there! But I never found her new place after that discovery.

We all have stashes. I have found that chocolate is the most popular food to hide or stash. I doubt anyone is surprised about that. But I have learned not to stash candy, especially chocolate, in my car's console. I put a candy bar in there a couple of days before driving down to Charleston. I forgot it was in there and parked in the sun. Have you ever tried to eat a melted chocolate candy bar while driving down the road? First, I had to open it with my teeth and literally squeeze the contents out of the wrapper. Then I had to pull over to clean up the mess I made. Needless to say, all that added to my travel time. Never underestimate a woman having a chocolate attack. And hang the consequences!

Some people have clothing stashes. They buy articles and hide them in the back of a closet but don't wear them for a while and then say, "No, this isn't new. I've had it for a while." Hmm.

A friend mentioned to me how she and her husband like a

certain cracker, and so when the crackers are low, she will hide a pack for herself in a special place, so she will never run out. I wonder if he does the same.

One sure place to hide goodies where they won't be found is at the back of the lowest shelf in the refrigerator. Even we females don't like looking there! The last time I looked there, I found a boiled egg and an apple that must have been there since the last time I cleaned the refrigerator. (And never you mind when that was.) Getting down on one's knees to look for goodies might discourage the most serious sweets "monster."

Now excuse me while I run to the store. I'm out of candy bars and I need a chocolate fix.

CHAPTER 30

I Have Changed

Help! Help! Somebody please help me. I have lost myself and am trapped in some old lady's body. I am even living in her home and eating her food.

I just went to bed one night, and when I woke up . . . I was somebody else. Before all this happened, I was younger, taller, and much thinner, and I sure looked better than this woman who's imprisoned me in her body. I read once that we are the sum total of all our experiences, and I believe she has had quite a few experiences. Somebody get me out of here!

Another thing: Where are my friends? I don't know these other people. They're really nice, but they look a lot like the woman who is holding me hostage. And the food! What has she been eating to make her look this way? I looked in this woman's refrigerator, and her food is boring. "Where's the beef?" All I see is fish and chicken. There are no preservatives in her food, and the way she looks, she needs all the preservatives she can get her hands on. Where does she keep her stash of potato chips? Why are there pill bottles on the counter instead of a cookie jar? All I can find that seems remotely good is some dark chocolate. I prefer milk chocolate! She doesn't even drink real milk. Almond and coconut milk, ugh.

She has notes everywhere. She even has one on the door going into the garage that says, "Got Keys, Phone, and Purse?" She also has a Senior Texting list she uses: LOL (Living on Lipitor), CTF (Clemson Tiger Fan), NPUB (Never Pass Up a Bathroom), PUBT (Passed Up Bathroom/Trouble), DTB (Don't Tell Your Brother), and KTF (Keep This in the Family). Oh, and from the looks of her calendar, she sure seems friendly with a lot of doctors.

UPDATE: I've had an epiphany since yesterday. A calmer head is prevailing, and I'm getting a funny feeling that I am not actually living in an alternate universe. This woman's life is really my life. But when did all of these changes take place? Where was I when the wrinkles came and gravity took over my entire body, starting with my face and working its way down?

When did I start needing higher wattage light bulbs? When did I start asking, "What did you say?" too often! I do remember thinking I should stop nodding and smiling when I didn't have a clue what the conversation was about or what I was promising to do. (This is what happens when you can't hear and don't want to acknowledge the hearing is going.)

Why is it so easy to cry when we are older? (Yes, men, you

do it too.) We are moved to tears when we see an abused dog or watch a funeral, even when we don't know the deceased. Yes, I cried watching Nancy Reagan's funeral. I was moved by the beautiful love story between her and her husband, former President Ronald Reagan.

We *are* the sum total of all our experiences, and by the time we retire we have had a continual flow of happy and sad ones. As a result, our hearts are more tender to suffering and the plight of other people, even those we don't know. We become more forgiving of others and more patient with lapses of memory and promises made and not kept because they were forgotten.

I'm glad I realized the woman in the mirror is still me. A little worn around the edges, maybe, but also a little wiser, and thank God, still useful in this ever-changing, topsy-turvy world we live in.

CHAPTER 31

Job Opening

Wanted: Looker, finder, rememberer, and reminder. Must have excellent eyesight with the ability to find lost items such as stylus pens, sunshades, cell phones, keys, just-purchased ink cartridges, reading glasses, passwords of accounts, notes of birthdays of family members, doctor appointments, warranties, and oven cleaner directions.

Must be athletic enough to climb up one or two steps of step-ladder to clean the top of the refrigerator and to reach the top of the bookcase to plug and unplug the router when the internet goes south or wherever it goes when it ceases to work. Must be agile and able to bend in the middle while searching under the front and back seats of the car for appointment cards, tubes of lipstick, mail, lost earrings, Wendy's coupons, and coins.

Must be technologically advanced enough to decipher messages on the computer such as "A plugin isn't working, the page is unresponsive, you can wait, or you can kill it." What?! Or "Aw snap, there was a problem, and we cannot open this document." Help.

Must be able to remember three items at a time from the grocery store, dollar store, and drugstore, and to never buy poppy seeds again and again for the one tablespoon needed for my favorite recipe. Poppy seeds, anyone?

Must stand next to me or behind me and repeat two times in my ear what people say as they introduce themselves and say their name. Sit next to me while I'm on the phone with my children to remind me when I've already told them some information before I start to tell it again. Don't let them know any information that might misconstrue my standing as a sharp parent, totally in control of all my faculties.

Since I'm type-2 diabetic, must have a strong personality to hide or eat the foods I buy in weak moments. Examples: potato chips, ice cream, french fries, and any cola drink, diet or other-wise, since I give my grandchildren grief about those things. Be a protector!

Tell me to "get over it" when I start on my yearly rampage about buying a used Road Trek and living and traveling in it for a year. Well, that would be on my bucket list if I had one.

Must be a positive person who always looks on the bright side and can forget unpleasant memories and can remind me of all the blessings I have on a daily basis.

Must be an athletic trainer and know how to spur me on to walk at least two miles every day and to tell me there are no excuses for not walking and that "sitting is the new smoking." (Yes, that's what I hear.)

If you can cover all these bases and remain sane, then you have a job. It may sound easy, but dealing with people as they age is not as simple as words on a paper.

The "and other duties" for this job may include explaining the Algebraic K-theory or the need for me to have Windows 10 on my computer. This should be done at two o'clock in the morning while I am still trying to go to sleep. These boring subjects should do the trick, and if it works, you will get a raise.

CHAPTER 32

Oops! Moments

We have all had moments when we wish the floor would suddenly open up and take us away from some embarrassing moments. I have had a few. Once on a business trip, I settled into my seat on the plane when I heard the flight attendant call my name to report to the front. Yep, I could not believe it, but I was on the wrong plane.

Years ago, when I was a member of a large women's group, we determined to have a fashion show and I helped plan the soirée. I called around making sure we had all the models we needed and helped secure clothing from upscale stores. After engaging a babysitter and dressing in my finest outfit, I arrived early to help. Not recognizing any cars in the parking lot should have put me on notice.

I entered the banquet room, expecting beautiful decorations only to see chairs on top of tables. It was the wrong week! I was so embarrassed I couldn't bring myself to tell my family what I did. I still cannot explain how I helped plan an event and got other people there on the right day, but not myself.

When I was eight years old, I visited my granddaddy overnight and had just gotten over a cold that left me with a hacking cough. So, Granddaddy put some clear liquid in a bottle the size of a large vanilla flavoring bottle, put white "rocks" in it so it wouldn't taste so bad, and told me to just sip it when I coughed—just a small sip.

Well, I still had the cough on Monday when I went back to school. Granddaddy never said a word about not taking the medicine to school. And I never told my mother I had it. Well, I was a hit with the big bullyboys on the school bus (the same ones who took my baseball cap). They passed the "Rockinrye" around until I told the bus driver they had my medicine. They gave it back but told the principal I had whiskey on the bus. I was called to the office pronto. He seized my medicine and gave me a "talking to" about bringing my granddaddy's medicine to school. My mother was a schoolteacher, and I think she was embarrassed more than I, since I just thought of the stuff in the bottle as "medicine."

All of this pales in comparison, however, to an experience I had years ago, when I worked in resource development for United Way in another town and managed certain accounts. There were several hospitals in town, but one hospital never participated in our campaigns. My assignment: meet with their personnel manager and ask if they would change their mind.

The appointment was scheduled for eight thirty on a Monday morning. Fully rested, having been on vacation the week prior, I had all my ducks in a row. My appointment book had gone with me to the beach, where I'd left it in the car (parked under a wonderful oak tree) under the driver's seat. Of course, I'd brought it with me to the appointment, since back then we didn't have cell phones for keeping track of our schedules.

Everything went very well with Gloria, the personnel manager. At the end of the appointment, she suggested, "Let's look at some dates for another meeting," so I took my appointment book out of my lap. When I opened it, a giant Charleston roach ran out across the desk and right into her lap. She screamed. I tried to smack the roach with my book. We never caught the roach, and I did not get the account. I tried to explain to her where my appointment book had been. It was no use. At least I wasn't fired over the incident. But it is right up there as the most embarrassing thing that ever happened to me.

CHAPTER 33

Back Then

When I was growing up over in Spartanburg County, we did some things that are unthinkable by today's standards. I bet some of you tackled and completed some tasks that would be foreign to your children and grandchildren, stuff they might be shocked or embarrassed to know.

One unimaginable thing we did was to tie Phoebe, the mentally disordered cow, in our side yard for all the world to see. I still have that memorable image in my mind. Even worse than that, her salt brick was there, also. When I told my mother I was so embarrassed and "would lose all my friends" because we had a cow in the yard, she explained that there was a shortage of pasture grass for her, and Phoebe was tied where the grass was lush, thick, and hard to cut since it was over the septic tank. So "Crazy Cow" became a self-propelled lawn mower. Of course, I made up all kinds of stories about why we had a cow tied in our side yard, but I'm sure all the neighbors knew it was a way to feed the cow in hard times. I actually didn't lose any friends for having a cow and salt brick in the yard, but at thirteen, I created a lot of drama about it.

I think about all the dogs our family had when I was growing up. I contrast the money it costs dog owners today to the costs of owning a dog back in the forties and fifties. When our dog was bitten by a snake or hurt in some way, there was one cure-all for any injury. Spent motor oil was poured on the affected area. And we never lost a dog to an injury or a snake bite. I am not advocating that kind of care today; I'm just stating facts about how it was back then. We only called a vet for large animals.

Some events happened on the farm more frequently than you can imagine. For instance, our mules would break out of the pasture and decide to run up and down the highway, go visit other farms, or just eat grass that was greener on the other side of another fence. They seemed to favor doing this funny stuff when it was dark and raining. Anyone who has ever chased an animal in those conditions knows it doesn't bring out the better side of humans or their vocabularies. Whoever coined the phrase "stubborn as a mule" was spot on with that description.

In the summer months we slept with only the screen latched on the front porch and all windows opened. We weren't robbed while we were sleeping, but we were robbed once when the house was all locked up and we were away for the day. That's when my mother bought a gun. (Heaven help us). We affection-ally called her "Sure-Shot Cecile," and she earned the name. My brother and I witnessed her shoot a stray dog that appeared to be rabid and another abandoned animal that was fighting our pets. Word got around that she was carrying "heat" and would use it. My brother and I never knew when and how she became knowledgeable about guns, but we ended up glad she did. No one bothered us after the word was out.

I am now thankful for the "back then" days. Sadly, most of our children/grandchildren will never know the freedom of sleep-ing with the windows open and only the screened porch latched, but maybe somewhere there is a cow tied in the yard and a teen-ager is embarrassed. All those "hardships" build character, and so goes life.

CHAPTER 34

Our Five Senses

Most days we are not even aware of our five senses that play such a key role in our daily lives. We take for granted our senses of smell, taste, sight, touch, and hearing. But if we lose one, then we realize the importance of each one. Our senses allow us to connect to the world.

Hearing. What are your favorite sounds? The music of the masters: Handel's *The Messiah*, "The Star-Spangled Banner," the sound of coffee brewing in the morning, the sound of the furnace on a cold day bringing warmth in and keeping the cold out? What about hearing the words "Tests show it is not cancer" or" I love you" for the first time, or the sound of feet running to meet you?

Touch. Can you believe how remarkably soft and smooth a baby's skin is? There is no other touch that gives the same feeling, especially when we are old and wrinkled. There are other touches that mean so much: a hug when you live alone, a handshake from a former foe, the healing touch when you are ill, or even a high-five when you didn't expect one?

Taste. I remember the first time I ate pizza. I knew I was hooked. It is one of my favorite foods, and the smell of garlic, cheese, and bread make me happy. Also, I never met a potato I didn't like, baked, creamed, fried, scattered, and covered: it doesn't matter. Potatoes are delicious.

Sight. The sight of seeing my newborn immediately after birth is one I've never forgotten. It is indelibly imprinted on my brain. And the ocean. Do you remember the first time you saw the ocean? Just the vastness was overwhelming to me. What about the glorious colors of fall foliage or seeing a beautiful flower garden? All of nature is magnificent to see.

Smell. Our sense of smell is linked closely to memory, probably more than any of our other senses, and can act as a trigger in recalling a long-forgotten event or experience. To walk into a home and smell the comforting aroma of beans and bread cooking makes me want to find a rocking chair and sit and breathe in that aroma while I reminisce of a simpler time. And there is the delicious smell of a homemade apple pie with cinnamon in it. Aaah! I, sadly, depend on Mrs. Smith's pies, but my daughter and daughter-in-law make homemade pies. I fell off the pie wagon sometime in the last decade.

Remember when we hung our sheets on the clothesline to dry? I loved the wonderful smell and the good feel of crisp, clean sheets on the bed. Remember the cross breezes when there was no air-conditioning and we lived with the windows open and could smell the outside? (Allergy sufferers are groaning about now.)

I love the aroma of coffee, the delicious, deep-brown wonder drug that makes my brain and other senses wake up. But I know for some people, Mountain Dew does the same thing—albeit without the aroma.

I am blessed that I still have all five senses working. I am grateful for that. But now, about this memory thing—it only works part-time. Oh, well, can't have everything, I guess.

CHAPTER 35

Scars

Most of us as adults have a few scars from childhood accidents or from surgery. The scars that can be seen are ones we can talk about, sometimes even brag about because they were trophies from playing sports or having fun in the snow or a hiking trip. We know the visible ones heal with the passage of time.

Little scars are just part of living in the world. We adjust very well to those. They make us more understanding and more attuned to the ebb and flow of life. Our scars are our own stories.

Of course, larger physical scars are more complex and take time to heal. Some never do. Some have to do with the loss of a limb. Those are the ones that keep us awake or attack us when we are down or discouraged. Large scars need cosmetic therapy sometimes, and we may need to talk about the trauma long after the initial injury happened.

Sometimes the most serious scars we carry are not physical ones. Stark nakedness will not show the deepest ones. They may mature us, teaching us about the world and about our fellow men. In many cases, they are the most permanent. Many of us grew up when the study of psychology was fairly new, and a lot was not known about the power of words. Remember the saying, "Sticks and stones may break my bones, but words will never hurt me." That is a lie. Words do hurt. Just ask someone who was taunted or called names all during childhood.

Ill-spoken words leave scars and wounds that can remain open for years. Things said on social media can cause enormous pain. People hiding behind computers and fake names say things to other people they would never say in a face-to-face situation.

Some scars result from someone playing recklessly with our hearts, and they can be life-altering, causing divorce and brokenness. Scars of the heart can't be seen, but we can and do recover from broken or scarred hearts. And our recovery is a testimony to our survival and can encourage others who have walked the same path to keep on keeping on.

Scars can build character. As children, when we first get a boo-boo, we learn we do recover, and it makes us more careful around things that can hurt us. So, our character—the way we think, feel, and behave—is formed as we learn not to do certain things, knowing we will get hurt.

How can we prevent scars? Some are inevitable as we navigate our lives; surgeries, cuts, and scrapes happen. We can watch our words, knowing words spoken in haste and in anger can scar others. It is well that we remember as we respond to others in social media that "The true test of a man's character is what he does when no one is watching" (John Wooden).

We can remember our own scars and what caused them and use those experiences to reduce the scar count among those who cross our path. Let's have a scar-free day today!

CHAPTER 36

The Struggle between Body and Mind

My mind tells me I can do everything—well, almost everything I could do when I was thirty. But my body is telling me something else. It's saying, "Oh, no you can't."

Some mornings I wake up and feel like I can conquer the day or at least seize the day, but later I realize my body has conquered me.

If I dare change my morning diet, I have gastric issues. If I cannot sleep after moving from bed to bed to sofa, I am "done in" the next day.

When I have more than two appointments on a given day, I'm wiped out by five o'clock.

My mind tells me I can shop with my daughter for hours, but my body says, "Don't you dare go to another store!"

And the last time I signed up for the two-year-old nursery during worship services, I needed to be wheeled out the door in a stroller myself.

Recently, I helped set up a yard sale, and the lifting and stooping seemed no problem until the next morning when I could hardly get out of bed. For five days, I wore a big, ugly back brace and looked like I should be working in a warehouse somewhere. But, hey, I'm not knocking it. The brace works.

Is this some kind of a bad joke the birthday fairy is playing on us? Because who ever said, "Getting old is not for sissies" knew what she was talking about. For example, I had a big memory slip three days ago and was so upset about it I planned to see a doctor to get an Alzheimer's test.

You've probably seen the commercial where the poor older woman can't find her keys and it turns out she's put them in the refrigerator. Well, I misplaced my phone last week. I searched every conceivable place and could not find it. I dreaded looking in the fridge for fear it was there. Thankfully, it was under a stack of papers I had overlooked.

But do I really want to know if Alzheimer's is coming on? Well, yes and no. Yes, so I can begin medicine, and, no, because I think I would be so depressed at the thought of having the disease that I wouldn't be good for anything.

So, you guessed it. I just chalked it up to "having a bad day." I will remain blissfully ignorant until another mental slip happens. If I forget where I live and can't find my way home from the grocery store, I'm calling. (If I can remember.)

My mother once went to a large shopping mall and entered the door nearest her car. An hour later, she left the mall through another door. She walked and walked, searching for her car. Finally, she went back inside the mall and told a security officer her car had been stolen. The officer was completely convinced, but as they were driving out of the parking lot on the way to the police station, Mama suddenly said, "Stop! There's my car. They must have brought it back!"

The moral of this story is, when you enter a big mall, take note of which door you enter, put a neon tennis ball on the radio antenna, or use your phone to take a picture of the lot number where you are parked. If you don't, you might wind up filing a stolen car report on a car that hasn't been stolen. Of course, if you can't remember where you left your phone . . . I can't help you.

CHAPTER 37

Taking Inventory

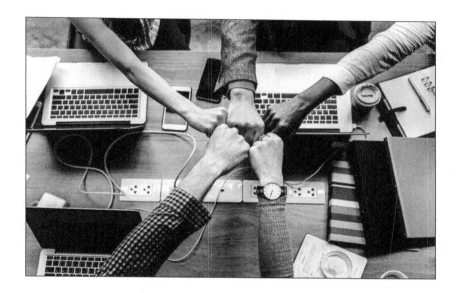

Have you ever thought about the people in your life who helped you get to where you are right now? There are always people who come into our lives at just the right time to move us ahead. It may have been in your childhood or when you were very young or at a difficult time in your life.

We all need others to come alongside us and give advice, friendship, the benefit of their life experiences, or even monetary help. We didn't get where we are by ourselves, although at some hard crossroads we may have felt nobody was there.

I've made a list of some people who helped me in different

ways, beginning in my childhood.

An aunt and uncle always took me on trips with them because I was my cousin's playmate, even though I was three years older than she. I was always on my best behavior on those trips. I might never have gotten out of Spartanburg County if they hadn't taken me with them. They broadened my world beyond the farm.

Once I had a teacher who believed in me and allowed me to write plays and "put them on" in English class. I also learned from another English teacher who never believed I wrote any of the essay assignments for her class. Because of that, I learned to keep on writing just to show her I could. So, both teachers played a part in moving me along. Sometimes even negative input can become a positive influence.

Once when I was desperate for a job, a minister I didn't know and had just met got down on his knees beside his desk and prayed fervently that I'd find one. I will never forget that prayer or that man. He was quite busy and knew I wasn't going to join his church, but he took the time to pray a beautiful and heartfelt prayer for a stranger. I got a job the next day.

The man who hired me didn't know anything about me and told me he had no openings and had no place to put me. He also said I needed to pass some tests before being hired. Then suddenly he asked me if I could be at work at eight o'clock the next morning. Unbelievable! And that job was a huge stepping stone to a better job later.

I found a condo that was close to my new job, but I didn't have money for the security deposit. The owner-agent rented the condo to me anyway. I eventually had the funds to pay the deposit, but I could hardly believe she allowed me to move in without it. I had never met her before and was a total stranger. It was an enormous help not to have to pay the extra money, and it allowed me to move forward with less worry.

Who has helped you get where you are right now? Some of the memories may be gloomy, but we grow from all our experiences and can thrive and even be appreciative for the times that were hard.

And remember, "Never underestimate the difference you can make in the lives of others. Step forward, reach out, and help. This week reach to someone that might need a lift" (Pablo). Your kindness could ease someone's discouragement or bring a smile to a worried face.

CHAPTER 38

The Strength of Love

SEPTEMBER 11, 2001
Forever In Our Hearts

A re you the wind beneath someone's wings? Or their cool breeze on a hot day or the sweet cream in their coffee? Or maybe their flower among the weeds? Will you be their fragrant rose among the thorns when they need you?

Will you be their joyful heart when theirs is so sad it is not working? Can you be their voice when sickness or pain stifles theirs? Do you feign deafness when they ask you the same question again and again and again? Can you be their soft touch when theirs has gone away? Will you sing their favorite song to them when they are unable to sing anymore?

Our memories make us who we are; some memories may be cloudy while others are tattooed on our hearts and lend us a loftiness of spirit and refreshment to our souls as we reflect on them. They give us hope and can rekindle the fires of times past when we were young and still dreamers. A certain song or the fragrance of a flower from years gone by can buoy our spirits and bring back other memories that are a part of who we are and where we came from.

As we grow and change, we become the authors of our lives by the attitudes we choose, the choices we make, and the chances we take as we write our own story. We can't change the winds that blow into our lives, but we can adjust the sails as we make this pilgrimage through life and wrestle with the ills of the world. But we do need others to be our refuge in darkness when adversities strike. And when they do come, we realize we are not an island unto ourselves, nor do we want to be. Life can be a struggle, and we strive to stay on the journey with everyone in one piece. Sometimes that doesn't happen. We find we need shoulders to cry on when we see our dreams fly away, and life seems an endless night and our hearts are bereft of feeling.

With the passage of fifteen years, Americans learned how important a sense of community can be. September 11 will forever live in infamy in this country, and we are reminded of the need for a healing balm of togetherness among us, the ones left in this republic. The passage of these years has made us more watchful to protect and be on watch for the evil that desires to destroy us. The fiber of this nation was challenged, but we are up to the challenge. The American can-do spirit that built this nation cannot be underestimated.

For the families who lost loved ones and the friends who lost friends, their lives changed forever. Golden dreams perished that day as children became orphaned. There was no daddy to earn a living or walk a daughter down the aisle for her wedding or to show a son how to throw a fastball. There wasn't a mama to teach the things that only mamas can teach.

After the attacks of 9/11, then-president George W. Bush said, "Terrorist attacks can shake the foundations of our biggest buildings, but they cannot touch the foundation of America. These acts shatter steel, but they cannot dent the steel of American resolve."

These words ring true in every area of our lives, and when the bad times come, there is strength in unity.

CHAPTER 39

Waiting for Mama

I would crawl underneath the camellia bush at the edge of the porch to wait for Mama to come home from work. It was a large bush with thick green leaves, and I could hide and not be seen by Mrs. Cudd, the housekeeper—only by my cat, Oatmeal. It was always cool, and Oatmeal would come and lie down in the damp dirt with me to wait. We would be very quiet. Soon Oatmeal would purr her happy sound and go to sleep. There were usually little ants (not the biting kind) and grasshoppers and sometimes a beetle, but I always felt safe with Oatmeal beside me.

She pounced on the grasshoppers, played with the beetles, and sometimes ate both!

Cars came and went down the dusty dirt road, tractors with hay bailers and flatbed wagons heavy with loads of hay pulled by horses. When the green hay was put up in the top of the barn, somebody always slept in the barn to make sure it didn't catch on fire during the night. Hay made me itch, and I was glad I was a girl and never had to sleep in the barn.

Mama's car was a gray 1944 Plymouth. I knew by the sound of the motor that it was Mama before she came in the driveway. Oatmeal and I would fly out from under the bush and welcome her home. I loved Mrs. Cudd, the housekeeper, but I was so happy when Mama came home. Our daddy had died years ago, so Mrs. Cudd stayed with my brother, Eric, and me while Mama worked.

Mama always had stories to tell about the school where she taught. The school was old and small with two classes in every room. Second and third grades were in the same room, second graders on one side and third graders on the other side. Bathrooms were outside in a little outhouse. When it rained and you had to go, you ran in the rain to the little house.

The first-grade classroom was also the lunchroom, and the aroma of cooking food being prepared fifteen feet away made it hard to concentrate—green beans, frying chicken, and baking biscuits!

When I was sick and Mrs. Cudd was away, I had to go to the old school with Mama and sit at the back of the classroom while she taught. I paid attention since she would call on me to make sure I was not sleeping.

It was a poor school and many children had shabby clothes and needed dental work and haircuts. Many grew up to do well, and some came to our house years later to thank Mama for teaching and caring about them.

One time, one of Mama's fifth-grade students found out where we lived and walked several miles to come see her. We were working in the yard that day and saw him coming from a distance. He an overweight boy of twelve with a full, round face. Perspiring profusely but with a grin of pure triumph, he greeted us with, "I just drank a big Pepsi-Cola and it is just a sloshin' aroun' in my belly." Mama was very gracious, did not try to correct any grammar during the visit. She even offered to drive him back home—which he refused. She often spent many extra hours at the school, and when the boy finally left, I heard her say under her breath, "Please, Lord, don't let the rest of them find me."

Oatmeal purred, and I smiled. Mama was home.

CHAPTER 40

Wanted: Computer Exorcist

It all started out when I tried to delete a contact and email conversations with a person who no longer uses her old email address. When I hit the delete button for my history with this old address, *pow*! Every one of my emails and my contact list were gone. Horrors, it can't be!

I tried every trick I had learned how to get my information back. But with everything I tried, I got the familiar *ding!* (the one that means "you can't do this") from the computer. I kept trying, and I tried to think rationally, but in my panic, I became mad that my deceased and very-computer-savvy husband was not here to get me out of the jam I had put myself in. He was used to my hissy fits when my technological skills were tested, and I wished I lived in a different time, when I didn't have to deal with all the technological frustrations that come from living in this century.

Well, I have no problem with one bit of technology: texting. So after I texted my daughter that I needed to send out a group e-mail but I had no e-mail, she remained calm, came over, and magically brought my email back to life. It looked totally different, but at least I had my email and my address book back. She left, and I proceeded to try to send out a group e-mail. I put the names in a box for team members, thinking that would be perfect. Suddenly, all the names disappeared. Undeterred, I entered the names one by one but misspelled the name of one addressee. Not one button I pushed would let me delete this wrong address. Whaaaa? I received an error message, so I assumed that the e-mail had failed to send to anyone.

In the meantime, I needed to print a word processing document. My trusty printer, which always works, decided I needed more fun in my life and would not print, saying I had no paper in the machine, which was a lie. I tried restocking the paper over and over. I pressed every button on my printer that I thought would make it know I had paper correctly installed—to no avail. Before I finished, I had my printer speaking French. Sorry, I'm not responsible anymore.

This time my son-in-law came and rescued me from myself. My computer is still not back to the way it originally was, but it works. And he couldn't believe I had my printer speaking French. (Don't ask.) He and my daughter fixed that, too.

At this point, I am emotionally shot from all this technological advancement we find ourselves enjoying. I have decided both my computer and my printer have been invaded by some evil spirits over which I have no control, and I am doubting my ability to survive the minutiae of this age.

You know what's funny about this whole scenario? The group e-mail I was attempting to send contained prayer requests from my Bible study group. By the time the list was finally sent, guess who needed prayer the most? God certainly has a sense of humor.

CHAPTER 41

What Happened to Sportsmanship?

This could be a grandmother's sociological rant because I am concerned about some of our young people and their reactions to life when something does not go the way they thought and planned.

When did it start, not being able to carry on with life when you have disappointments? This behavior of some college students being so upset that the college has to call in therapists, and animals to pet, and coloring books to relieve their terrible stress and the disappointment of their candidate losing. How absolutely beyond the pale is this behavior? Think about it: their fellow millennials are fighting in Afghanistan and Iraq and other dangerous places where they can easily die, and their peers are having to pet animals and color in coloring books because they are so stressed out about a political election. When questioned, many of these weeping college kids admitted they didn't even vote!

Did it all start when we gave trophies to kids on sports teams for just showing up? Was it when everybody got a trophy so everything would be equal and all would go away winners? Did it start when kids were socially promoted? What did we parents do to turn out such children behaving like this because their team lost?

Is it because many children have helicopter parents and phones at school so they can call every time class changes just to check in or when something is going on in the news that upsets them and they need reassuring? Is this why some young married women feel the need to call their mother several times a day? Can no one make a decision on their own anymore? Cell phones, email, Facebook, Twitter, and texting are good ways to keep in touch, but is it keeping us from using our own wits? And do we need to get everybody's opinion when we have a decision to make? Are we still capable of thinking for ourselves?

Did all this start with the self-esteem emphasis a few years ago when having high esteem was more important than learning what was in your books? Something had to happen to turn some of our young people into bad sports and sore losers.

Can you imagine if our generation reacted violently to an election we didn't like? Can you picture us breaking windows and rioting in the streets? I can't imagine it, primarily because we had a tough time just living and having food on the table. Destroying someone's property was foreign to most of us, and also our mamas and daddies would have come out into the street, dragged us home, and made us wish we had not been involved in such craziness. Our families would have been embarrassed, and our friends wouldn't have wanted to have anything to do with us anymore because we were acting like hooligans and hoodlums blocking traffic, filled with people trying to get to work.

Where are the parents of these street rioters? Shouldn't their children be in class or on a job? Who is keeping them up? Somebody must buy them food. When will this foolishness stop?

We just need to pray for our country.

CHAPTER 42

Why Did We Do It?

The things we do to ourselves to make life harder are folly. Things like eating spaghetti while wearing a white shirt or setting a glass of tea too close to the computer keyboard. Yep! It happened. We do things like not allowing enough time to get to an appointment and finding ourselves driving behind a slowpoke retiree on his way to eat breakfast with his ROMEO (Retired Old Men Eating Out) group at Hardee's. It's not his fault you are going to be late.

A friend told me about her neighbor who decided to eat some of his daughter's Halloween candy. He had never eaten a Sugar Daddy but loved caramel. He was home alone. The telephone rang, but when he tried to answer it, he found the sucker was stuck to both upper and lower dentures. He tried pulling. Nothing worked. He tried pulling both plates out, but that made matters worse. The person calling thought the man was having some sort of episode because he was unable to speak and making frantic guttural noises. Being a neighbor, he quickly came over to the man's house, fearing the worst. Between the two men, they finally got him unstuck. But why did he do it?

Recently I went on a hike to White Mountain. When we stopped for a bathroom break, I stuck my aviator sunglasses in the front of my shirt. When I leaned over to flush the commode, my sunglasses fell in. It was one of those moments where I was faced with an important choice: put my hand in this public toilet or walk out as if I didn't know anything about those glasses (which would have stopped up the plumbing). I reached in, pulled them out, and quickly put them in the trashcan. I washed my hands as well as I could. Double yuk! I needed more soap and hotter water. Well, I should have worn my industrial sunglasses from the ophthalmologist, but I wanted to look good and not like I had just had cataract surgery. Cataract surgery is how I got the industrial ones! That's what I get for trying to be cute and not old. "Pride goeth before . . ." You know the rest.

This next "why did we do it?" usually happens when we are distracted doing something like packing the car to go on a trip. The item we don't want buried underneath clothes or in a suit-case, we put on top of the car—items like our purse, lunch, a latte, or a new pair of shoes we want to wear when we arrive. Oh no, not my shoes. Why did I do it?

The very day you think you are not going out of the house, you suddenly realize you need something important from the grocery store. Your hair needs shampooing, your shirt has a stain in front, and you have on your yard shoes and no makeup. You are only going to get one item, Right in and right out. But as you go in the door, the neighborhood fashion plate is leaving the store, and she tries to engage you in a conversation when all you want to do is disappear. Why do we do it?

We do it because we are human and what we learn from history is that we do not learn from history. So keep doing some of this stuff so the rest of us won't feel like we are the only blunderers.

CHAPTER 43

Your Joy

What brings you joy? How do you find it if you have lost it? Some things we must do every day, just because we are alive and kicking, don't bring us joy because they are repetitive and ordinary. But turn that around: there can be joy in knowing what your life will be like day to day. Refugees who have lost the sameness of everyday life would be thrilled to get back to their same old routine. Joy is a matter of perspective.

Most of us have some people in our lives who exhibit joy. These are people who seem to live above the circumstances of age and their situations. I have some friends who are ninety-plus years old and yet have a zest for life and are still interested in what is going on in the world. They don't dwell on what is wrong with the world but rather what is right. Being in their company gives me joy because they are content and at peace.

The things that give us joy change as our life situations change. I am thinking of widowhood. When we lose a spouse or endure other misfortunes, we must reinvent ourselves and find joy in different ways. Yes, change is hard, but we must learn to embrace it.

I get joy from walking with friends, and it is easier to get up early and walk when you have others to whom you are accountable. Other simple joys can't be overlooked. Old movies, beautiful music, cold bottled water, mechanical pencils all over the house, pizza, and flowers: all these things give me joy. Even cold pizza with good coffee for breakfast is joy for me.

Looking for joy causes us to reexamine how we spend our time. Do you still feel joy being a member of the same club for years, or do you need to find a new group? Are you still compatible with the same people you've been friends with for twenty years? If they bring joy into your life, stay. If not, find joy with another group or form your own group. It's—*gasp*—OK.

Experiencing joy can mean changing some routines, like going to a new vacation spot instead of the same place you've gone for a decade. It is especially true when your life situation changes. There comes a time when we all need to make some new memories. Is there something you always thought you would enjoy doing once you retired or the children were gone? Learning to build furniture, playing a musical instrument, going on a mission trip, or camping? Then do it. Do it!

Joy doesn't just jump into your lap. Sometimes you need to take inventory and decide what makes you joyful. Being thankful is one way to think about joy. It helps to write out all the good things in your life and to also list what no longer is joyful or useful. If your "stuff" no longer gives you joy, get rid of all or at least some of it. Pare down. It can be very freeing because the more stuff we have, the more stuff we must dust, wash, store or move. And don't plan on your children wanting a lot of your stuff; they really don't want to polish, wash, dust it, either.

And remember: joy and happiness are not the same thing. Happiness is fleeting and temporary. It's great while it lasts, but joy goes much deeper and comes from the heart, which is where our treasure is.

The Dutch Catholic priest, theologian, and writer Henri Nouwen once wrote, "Joy does not simply happen to us. We have to choose joy and keep choosing it every day."

ACKNOWLEDGMENTS

Thank you to Steven Bradley for allowing me the opportunity of writing a column for the *Seneca Journal*.

To Shirley McAlister for editing the columns for the *Journal*.

Also, to the faithful readers of *Homespun*.

To my friend, Dr. Jerdone Davis, for her encouragement and expert technical assistance. You were instrumental in getting this book to publication.

To Beth Brawner for her photographs.

To my patient son-in-law, Gregg Eargle, for his technical assistance.

And to my friends and family who gave me fodder for *Homespun*. You are priceless.

ABOUT THE AUTHOR

Born in the South Carolina upstate and raised on a family farm, Elaine Cameron is a true daughter of the South, a free-range child who has been writing essays all her life. She has a knack for seeing humor in the everyday and for saying what everyone else is thinking. A mother of two and a grandmother of three, she resides in Clemson with Sir George of Bayberry, the Cat.

Made in the USA
Columbia, SC
18 October 2021